The Grown-Up's Guide to Living in France

The Grown-Up's Guide to Living in France

ROSANNE KNORR

TEN SPEED PRESS
BERKELEY / TORONTO

To John
for planting the seed of an idea
and to the Ten Speeders who helped bring it to fruition.
Mille mercis

A Kirsty Melville Book

1🠒

Ten Speed Press
P.O. Box 7123
Berkeley, California 94707
www.tenspeed.com

Distributed in Australia by Simon and Schuster Australia, in Canada by Ten Speed Press Canada, in New Zealand by Southern Publishers Group, in South Africa by Real Books, in Southeast Asia by Berkeley Books, and in the United Kingdom and Europe by Airlift Book Company.

Cover design by Kathy Warinner
Cover illustration by Kathy Warinner
Interior design based on a design by Laura Lind Design

Library of Congress Cataloging-in-Publication Data on file with the publisher.

ISBN 1-58008-145-2

First printing, 2000
Printed in Canada

1 2 3 4 5 6 7 8 9 10 — 04 03 02 01 00

Contents

Acknowledgments

In my own life here, I owe thanks to dozens of people who helped me adapt to France. Many of them also helped with this book. This includes Americans (and those who purport to speak something close, the Brits, Australians, and New Zealanders) who shared stories and tips on adapting and finding the best plumber. French friends patiently explained the countless details and reasons behind the differences in culture.

A few in particular stand out. A special *merci* to Amanda Abernathy; Judith Bluysen; Betsy and John Braden; Scott, Sara, and Nicole Corregan; Annick Couritas; Pam and Steve de Lyra; Marie-France and Michel Desnoulez; Patricia Elvee; Adrian Leeds; Margo Milner; Jan and Earl Palmeter; Jill Steenhuis-Ruffato; and Dorothy van Schooneveld.

Note to Readers

We've made every effort to ensure that the information in this book is accurate. However, France is a grande and complicated country, with countless regional customs and distinctions. Even within the same region, regulations and typical procedures can vary or change.

When planning your sojourn, use this book as a jumping-off point. But don't jump too far without considering your specific needs and lifestyle. This book cannot substitute for the professional assistance of accountants, lawyers, tax experts, travel agents, and other specialists, who can advise you based on your particular situation at the time you make a transition to France. As with any major life change, investigate fully and carefully. Neither the author nor the publishers can be responsible for decisions made solely on the basis of reading this book without professional guidance.

If, in the course of your planning, you discover additional information, or would like to point out corrections or make comments for inclusion in future editions, please contact the author in care of the publisher.

Introduction

The runaway adventure began with *The Grown-Up's Guide to Running Away from Home,* which provides inspiration and information about preparing for long sojourn or retirement overseas.

It was a good beginning. In fact, the dream apparently took hold so well that many of you requested information on running away to specific destinations.

So we're taking off with my personal favorite, France. This country is so charming, varied, and totally *agréable* for art, history, and cuisine that it can fill years with pleasure. No wonder it's a runaway's dream location!

The Grown-Up's Guide to Living in France is designed to provide the flavor and the facts that will enable you, first of all, to imagine what daily life would be like for you in France, and secondly, to start your adventure off on the right *pied,* should you decide to implement this change in lifestyle.

About Prices and Exchange Rates. The prices in this book will give you a general idea of the costs of French products and services—in both francs and dollars. However, exchange rates fluctuate minute-by-minute. In the years I've been in France, the exchange rate has ranged from 5.4 to 6.7, so I chose a middle course of six francs per U.S. dollar as the conversion factor. If the franc rises or falls greatly from six francs to the dollar, use the current exchange rate to determine current dollar values.

About French Terms. French translation of words related to each topic are scattered throughout the book. These are not in any way intended as an attempt to teach you the French language. For that, you'll need to study grammar, pronunciation, and much more vocabulary. However, the words chosen in this book are specialized terms that don't get covered in beginning French classes, but that will come in handy for the daily needs of a person moving to France.

People who are already conversant in French will notice that I committed the mortal sin of dropping the required article (*le, la,* or *les*), which designates the feminine, masculine, and plural of nouns. This was done to facilitate the alphabetical listings, which otherwise would appear to have words all starting in *l.*

French teachers, please forgive me.

Enough about practicalities…now start imagining your new lifestyle in this land of wine and sunflowers, and discover what it takes to make that dream a reality. You may someday wake up and discover that you are actually living the good life in *la belle France.*

I wish you *bonne chance!*

The Grown-Up's Guide to Living in France

1
Vineyards and Castles and Cheese, Oh My!

TOTO, I HAVE A FEELING WE'RE NOT IN KANSAS ANYMORE.
—Dorothy, *The Wizard of Oz*

France. Just six letters conjure up a kaleidoscope of romantic, whirling images known by tourists the world over: Gargoyles peering over Notre Dame's flying buttresses; the neck-craning height of the Eiffel Tower; sublimely decorated *châteaux* filled with priceless art and antiques; elegant people sipping wine in sidewalk cafés; elaborate five-course dinners served on Limoges plates; and buttery croissants heaped on trays in a bakery window.

Can you imagine living in France? Do Americans here really live like this year round? Well, yes and no. Those of you who succeed in setting up a French life outside the tourist bus will soon discover that the magic remains, though it shifts focus. Like living anywhere else, living in France becomes a part of your daily life—and that's exactly what makes it even better than those glossy tourist brochures.

Tourist activities are temporary clicks in a two-week existence. Living in France on a daily basis is the unedited and long-playing version, enabling you to create your own treasured moments, which are no less vivid, but which are resounding in joyful simplicity.

The Eiffel Tower? If you live in Paris, its friendly presence hovers over the Champs de Mars when you walk your dog and meet friends on a sunny afternoon. The Louvre? Everyone agrees it's too grand to take in on one trip. Well, you don't have to. Return on rainy days or whenever you want to peruse special exhibits at your leisure.

Do you prefer a country lifestyle? Live in France throughout the year and you'll have time to notice the exact day that the vast fields of *colza* turn spring into a sunny drift of yellow more vivid than the ubiquitous posters of sunflowers. Take a last-minute trip to the Atlantic coast just to enjoy the fresh seafood or drive down to the Dordogne because you're in the mood for *foie gras*.

Spend a long summer vacation at the beach or take your holidays on a daily basis, attending the countless musical and artistic events, antique shows, and food fairs that fill the French calendar.

It's fall? Grab your bike for a tranquil ride past the parallel rows of grapevines, plump with purple fruit. When the weather cools, discover December's Christmas market in Strasbourg, where you can stock up on holiday decorations and warm body and spirit with hot mulled wine and Alsatian cuisine.

Throughout the year, shop the market stalls for whatever farm produce is currently in season—fat white asparagus, juicy cherries, bright red tomatoes, succulent melon. And don't forget to pick up a bunch of colorful flowers to adorn the table.

Yes, life in this divine hexagon offers an array of sensory pleasures. It's no wonder that people who've visited here get more stars in their eyes than Orion at the thought of living in France.

Thousands of Americans have made the dream a reality, often surprising themselves by staying longer than they first planned. My husband and I began by saying, "We'll live there for five months." That was more than three years ago. Our experience is similar to many other American expatriates here, who thought they were arriving for an extended vacation and ended up extending the experience into a lifestyle.

France draws nationalities from around the world, including tens of thousands of Americans. Official U.S. State Department records show that there are more than 90,000 of us here, though the truth is that number is just the tip of the *croissant*. The State Department admits it can't keep track of Americans who don't register at the embassy—and many don't.

We feel at home in Europe, as much or more so than in America.
We were swimming against the tide of materialism just when
we wanted to simplify and get back to basics.
—Betsy and John, the Dordogne

MAGIQUE MOMENTS

Exactly why do these Americans (as well as Brits, Australians, and other English speakers) hang their *chapeaux* in France? This is a question we're asked often, mostly by the French, who can't imagine why an American would want to uproot themselves from the rising star, the United States.

Lifestyle is the first word most Americans living in France use to explain their decision. Paris rush hours aside, France offers a tranquil existence, one that encourages people to relish their daily *baguette*, appreciate each tiny millimeter as grapes grow plumper on the vine, and spend time feeding friendships with daily doses of conversation and long lunches.

The French excel at enjoying the moment. They even have a phrase that expresses it perfectly: "*On doit profiter.*" This "profiting" has nothing to do with your wallet. It indicates that one should profit from a sunny day, friends, or the bouquet of a good wine.

France has long inspired artists and art lovers to find their muses here. Art is found around every corner in France, not just in the tourist meccas. Stroll the streets of even the smallest village and you'll marvel at the history and beauty around each corner. This country is proud of its artistic accomplishments and displays them for the world, whether it be at the world-famous Louvre or the smallest off-the-beaten-path chapel.

Seeking out all that culture takes energy, and one develops an appetite. Even the most avid art buff will admit that the *cuisine* draws them to France as much as Monet and Cézanne. Taste buds here enjoy the world's finest dining room, which spreads its varied buffet from cream-rich Normandy to tomato-based dishes of the Mediterranean, from the Germanic accents in Alsace to the rich *foie gras* of the southwest. And everywhere, simply everywhere, there are cheeses. Rich and flavorful, they provide 365 reasons to applaud the traditional cheese course.

The language, though a major source of complaints for those attempting to learn it, is also one of France's glories. Yes, it initially seems like an incomprehensible *mélange* of vowels that makes each sentence sound like one massively long word. But the cadence of French makes even ordering a ham sandwich sound like the most eloquent and loving prose. (Well, considering the superior ham, perhaps it is.) Americans who take the time to learn the language eventually notice that the romantic, though formerly unintelligible sounds sort themselves into meaningful phrases.

Then there are the people who speak this poetic language fluently, the French themselves. Some recent newspaper surveys contend that English-speaking tourists "love France but hate the French." Those, sad to say, are tourists caught in a culture gap. In living here, those "arrogant" French turn out, in fact, to be charming and polite. The person who delves deeper than a carry-on suitcase learns that the French are warm and welcoming to those who take the time to understand their culture—and to participate in it.

Even the inevitable presence of poodles, terriers, and a Toto or two sitting under the tables in *les cafés* soon becomes part of the delightful difference that is France.

A magnificent ambiance sets France apart from the humdrum world and is a direct result of France's pride and determination to maintain its unique culture. It will fight tooth and nail to keep its language pure and its cheese unpasteurized. Because both are better that way.

That, in a hazelnut shell, is what makes France a lovely place to explore long-term—and an even better place to live. If the magic is starting to sink into your soul, you'll soon know it. If you're reading this book, then most likely the process has already begun. You're curious to know what life would be like in France. You want to try it, but like most of us, you have your doubts—and your questions. What is the lifestyle really like? Is it hard to learn French? Can I get a visa? How do I find somewhere to live? Can I afford it? Can I take my pets?

The prospect at first seems daunting, but living in France is certainly possible. You may enjoy finding your own little corner of this hexagon to settle down for a lengthy and captivating sojourn.

With that in mind, this book will introduce newcomers (and wannabees) to the more important details of daily life. Don't look for listings of tourist sites here; bookstore and library shelves are packed with books suggesting hotels and restaurants and sites to see. What you will find are impressions and information gathered from my experience and from talking with other Americans living in France—information that it took many of us years to discover by hit or miss, but which will give you a shortcut to settling in.

This book will help you imagine what your daily routine would be like and decide if living in France—temporarily, long-term, or for retirement—would be to your liking. If you choose to move here, I hope the book provides the basic background needed to plan your stay, set up your new home, understand the way of life, and adapt successfully to this lovely country.

May your experience be truly *magnifique*.

I don't regret a moment of our new life,
and we still find time for that occasional six-hour lunch.
—Margot, the Drôme Provençale

2
French Beauty Spots

THE COUNTRY IS LYRIC, THE TOWN DRAMATIC.
WHEN MINGLED THEY MAKE THE MOST PERFECT MUSICAL DRAMA.
—Henry Wadsworth Longfellow, *Kavanagh*

A geography teacher would explain that France is the largest country in Western Europe. Believe it. Tourists who attempt to cover France in the ten-day, see-it-all-or-bust trip fail to unearth the multifaceted richness of this country. Lucky is the person who lives here and has the time to explore.

Note that I did not say *fully* explore. Seeing all that France has to offer, even the highlights, is virtually impossible within a lifetime. France is more than voluminous; it's endlessly varied. France provides diversion aplenty for anyone fortunate enough to be here long enough to wander without worrying about catching the tour bus for a quick return trip.

The only difficulty lies in determining where you want to settle for the long term, because each spot offers something special. Of course, you could always try serial living, or moving from one region to another. Don't laugh. Many an expat has considered it. But in most cases, they've settled into one life in a favorite spot and traveled to the other areas, using the excellent train or road system.

VARIÉTÉ IS THE SPICE OF LIFE

Is France truly just one country? You might not think so if you arrived unknowingly amid the Spanish architecture of Perpignan, or stopped for lunch in Nice, with its Italian-accented restaurants serving pasta and pizza.

Strasbourg's half-timbered houses could be equally at home in Germany (which, in a way, they were, since the area has bounced back and forth between France and Germany for centuries).

Then there's the North African–influenced Marseilles, the Celtic traditions of Brittany, the Basque traditions to be found along the Spanish border. These varied regions, and countless others, have maintained their historical roots, providing fascinating perspectives in architecture, new tastes in food and drink, and excursions into different dialects and lifestyles.

In physical terrain and climate, France offers virtually every possibility, except for cactus-filled deserts or humid rain forests. The country stretches from the rough-hewn cliffs of the northern Atlantic shores to the stony beaches of the palm-lined Mediterranean. You can settle in a quiet village in the back country of Haute Provence or brave Alpine mountain peaks. (Though unless you're a mountain goat, you won't want to live on Mont Blanc; it's the highest peak in Europe.) You can ponder life in a quiet hamlet or place yourself in the midst of Parisian grandeur.

DECIDING FACTORS

Select an area or areas that interest you, whether for culture or climate or terrain. Then study up on them to narrow the list. Contact local tourist bureaus for information. They will often provide helpful information such as lists of local real estate agents. Order the local paper or check it out on the Internet. (Many of the locales are going high-tech these days, even some of the seemingly pastoral ones.) As you narrow down the choice, you can begin using increasingly specific criteria.

The Internet is terrific for researching destinations and talking to people who live in or have traveled to the region you're exploring. Check message boards for France. Although most are for people going for short stays, occasionally you will find people who are moving there or who have visited often enough to provide impressions of specific areas. Don't count on just one person's impression, however, as that person may have just had a bad day—or an especially good one. Count on an accumulation of impressions from different sources to improve your chances of making the right decision.

America Online has a member directory, which allows you to check for members who live in a particular area. Put France in the country block, then the name of a city or region you want to know more about. You'll get a list of members who noted that area as their home. Contact them and politely explain that you're interested in moving there, and ask whether they would mind if you asked some questions. Most people will be pleased to help.

Incidentally, phrase your questions in French if you can or choose user names that sound Anglo/American.

City Mouse or Country Mouse?

Everyone has different priorities when choosing a place to live. France is so diverse, you'll need to decide what style of life you want to have before settling somewhere. Here are a few considerations:

Access

- Is it easy to reach an international airport for trips to the United States? Or visits from family and friends?
- Is the location convenient to train services? Is it the regional train or the high-speed TGV?

Climate

- Are you a snow bunny or a sun seeker? Check out the climate in all seasons.

Health Care

- How close are you to good medical care?
- If you have a condition requiring a specialist, are you near a city with necessary services?

Culture and Leisure

- Do you want the advantages of city life, such as museums, libraries, theaters, and English-language movies?
- Would you prefer tranquillity or a sports-oriented existence in the country?
- Can you play the sports you enjoy nearby?

English Speakers

- Do you want to be near other expatriates, or would you like to immerse yourself in the French culture? Or a bit of both?
- Are you willing to speak only French? Or do you want to be in a tourist area where it's more likely that shopkeepers will speak some English?

Cost of Living

- Can you afford to live comfortably in the city or region?
- Is the average housing affordable and to your liking?
- Can you afford the amount of space you require, or are you willing to downsize?

Crowd Control

- Do you want a pastoral existence, or do you prefer bright lights?
- Is the area overrun with tourists in peak months—the beach in summer or the ski slope in winter?

Potential for Employment

- If you need to earn a living or supplement your savings, does the area offer employment possibilities?

Make your plans known and you're bound to uncover people who know the area. In the best case, you'll create a base of friends overseas before you even set foot in France!

REGIONS

A comprehensive examination of the entire country would take volumes. Books fill the shelves of your local bookstores and library on every magnificent detail of France. You'll see picture-perfect scenes from tourist agencies, the ones that make you ache with longing to be in the scene. These touring facts can be helpful to your dream but they're readily available; I won't repeat those facts and figures.

Here are a few areas that Americans have found to be great places to live. These facts are presented, not from a tourist point of view, but from an American runaway's experience. When you live somewhere, you'll want vital facts on the weather, terrain, culture, food, the personality of the area and its people, as well as your chances of being accepted by the local people and finding compatible English-speaking friends.

Most of the areas covered are sections of the country, but one city makes the list. It's so magnificent, extraordinary, and every other grand adjective you can name, we'll begin there.

It starts with a first visit and you fall in love with the city.
Then you return and return again until one day you realize you
absolutely must spend a year here, which turns into two, three...
and before you know it, you're entrenched.
—Adrian, Paris

CITY LIGHTS

Paris

Who hasn't been enthralled by Paris? Who hasn't taken one look and surrendered, heart and soul, to her allure? (Well, okay, there is that tourist who didn't check the metro map at rush hour and asked a tired, surly commuter directions to Montmartre.) For the most part, however, Paris is truly a *grande dame*, sophisticated and charming, wealthy, but amazingly down-to-earth too. Large as the metropolitan area is, Paris has a city core that's strollable and neighborhoods that are like villages in which residents know the local butcher and baker and bistro owner.

Living in Paris puts all that Paris offers at your doorstep. Cultural events are in abundance, with access to the Louvre, the Musée d'Orsay, the Opéra, and hundreds, no thousands, of other opportunities to discover art, music, and theater.

For an American living in Paris, you'll be able to take advantage of English-speaking clubs and classes. The American Library and English-language bookstores provide handy reading material in your native language. Even English-language movies, which in many other parts of France are dubbed into French, are found in movie theaters throughout the city—and are practically wall-to-wall on the Champs-Elysée.

Paris is the place where you can assuage your craving for Tex-Mex or American-style fast food, with the fact your hamburgers are washed down with wine being the only reminder of the location. In Paris, you will also find quaint bistros and the world's top chefs.

Paris is the center of business and study in France with international corporations and schools adding an influx of English-speaking business-people and students. It's the cosmopolitan center as well; Parisians are said to look down on their provincial brothers, even while counting the days till *les vacances* when they can get out of the city and join them.

Paris is a hub for travel, whether you want to travel within France or internationally. If your appetite is for an environment that offers a never-ending round of activity and possibilities, Paris is the choice spot. Just make sure you have a good job or an inheritance. Living in Paris is costly, and to afford it, most people step down their expectations. A three-bedroom home in a less-costly rural area costs about the same as a one-bedroom walk-up apartment in Paris. Then again, when Paris is just outside the door, who wants to stay inside?

THE SOUTHEAST

Provence

It hardly seems necessary to explain Provence. The area's made the best-seller list for years, thanks to Peter Mayle. It's popular and populated by Americans and Brits, which makes some people choose the area almost reflexively. Indeed, the area is truly beautiful. Provence emits a golden glow, quite literally, as the sun reflects gently off ocher hills and stone walls. Cypresses stand tall and slender, while plane trees cast plump canopies of shade against summer heat. My favorites, though, are the sculptural, gnarled olive trees, which bear their fresh gray-green harvest. Purple lavender and red poppies punctuate all that dusky gold and green.

Artists have always been attracted to Provence (it's the light, they say). Today Americans and Brits by the score live here, so you'll have a built-in source of English speakers. Aix-en-Provence is, though not large, probably the most popular spot for English speakers, who offer ready-made access to the community and integration into the lifestyle. Not that Aix is the end-all; you'll find English speakers scattered thickly in the hill towns through-out Provence.

The food here is a healthy combination of fruits and vegetables, with fewer of the rich, cream-based sauces of the north. Meals are complemented by tomato-based sauces with garlic, and fresh fruits, such as cantaloupes and cherries.

Tourism is a major force in Provence, which is a disadvantage for residents during the prime summer season. Summer is also the hottest time, and for some, that can be unbearable without a cooling pool, as air conditioning is rare in most of France. Spring and summer are the best seasons. Most people assume that Provence is warm in winter, because it's in the south. Don't count on it. Snow is unusual but the frigid *mistral* sweeps from the north in wintry blasts.

Côte d'Azur

Unless you have a fetish for traffic jams, avoid the Riviera like a swarm of jellyfish in summer. It once took us an hour to go five miles along the coast road from Nice airport to Cannes. I shudder to think of it even now. But if you love popular places, palm trees, and beautiful people, many of whom, including the female half, go topless on the beaches, then the Côte d'Azur may be your place in the sun.

Expatriates who live in the Côte d'Azur cluster along the eastern coastline, especially in the Cannes and Nice areas, although inland at Sophia Antipolis, the international corporations, such as IBM, create virtual suburbs of English-speaking expatriates.

Due to tourism, English is heard often, and it's spoken by the smart gallery owners, restaurateurs, and shopkeepers, who recognize the benefits of catering to the influx of moneyed visitors.

The real estate in Côte d'Azur soars as high as the market will bear. A tiny studio apartment, which offers a balcony-sized peek at the Mediterranean, will cost as much as a four-bedroom house almost anywhere else in the country. In the hills behind Cannes and Nice, prices are a bit more reasonable but only in relationship to the inflated prices of the coastline.

Nice's international airport is convenient for flights directly to and from the United States. Fast TGV trains connect Paris to Avignon, Marseilles, Nice, Cannes, Antibes, and Menton. Towns are strung out along the Riviera, but crowds pack the roads and high-rises. Smaller villages in the hills are away from the coast but also away from the hubbub. Even these, however, are jam-packed in summer.

The climate is hot in the summer. If you're near the Mediterranean, you can take a dip, but most people consider access to a pool essential. If you can't afford your own, try for an apartment complex that includes one. You won't be swimming in winter, but the area around Nice and environs is protected from the *mistral* that otherwise plagues Provence, so winters are milder and spring comes sooner here than in most areas of France.

We discovered Brive by accident, since we had a French friend who
moved back from the States. We spent a month in her centuries-old farmhouse
and decided to settle here. Our new home is fifteen minutes outside Brive,
in a hamlet that numbers thirty-two when we're here!
—Betsy and John, the Dordogne

THE SOUTHWEST

Dordogne

The Dordogne region has lured mankind for 100,000 years. The Lascaux and Les Eyzies-de-Tayac caves are here, where primitive man made his mark, literally, on the walls. The Dordogne is also home to numerous Brits and a few Americans who are attracted by its lush landscapes and sumptuous *foie gras*.

This section of southwest France is named for the Dordogne River that runs through it; however, it also encompasses several different *départements*, such as Lot, Lot-et-Garonne, Gers, and Tarn. And you'll also hear it called Périgord.

The Dordogne and other river valleys display cliff-side vistas that are nothing short of spectacular. The area is largely farmland and always seems to be bright green with rolling meadows. There are *châteaux* and charming villages to explore, and dark forests, where people seek those priced-like-gold mushrooms called truffles. If that's not enough rich eating for you, serve up some of the local *foie gras*, the melt-in-your-mouth duck or goose liver. Nothing tastes better with it than the sweet white Monbazillac wine of the region.

Medieval Sarlat is a seventeenth-century town of ocher stone and ornamented houses that are typical of the historic Dordogne. Brantôme, called the Venice of Périgord, is another charming town; it is situated on the river Dronne.

Though not completely out of reach, the Dordogne is far enough away from Paris and the chichi importance of the Riviera to have maintained reasonable prices in housing. The climate is typically mild in the Dordogne, but expect cold winters and hot, dry summers.

Languedoc-Roussillon

The southwest of France borders Spain and the Pyrénées, which explains the area's Spanish flavor. You may even hear Catalan, the language of Barcelona, spoken in the Basque area. The name of the area comes from the term *langue d'oc*. The inhabitants, influenced by Catalan, originally said *oc* for yes, not *oui*.

The magnificent city of Toulouse is the fourth largest city in France. Though Toulouse is located on the northern limits of this region, it bears mentioning. Known for its red brick, which gives the city a sunset glow all day long, Toulouse is cosmopolitan and prosperous, because of its emphasis on technical expertise. The Concorde jet was created in Toulouse. Shopping, though not on the grand scale of Paris, is popular, due to the high quality of the boutiques.

Just north of Toulouse is Albi la Rouge. Yes, it's called red for the same red-glowing brick. The town is smaller than Toulouse but charming and close to the "big city." It's the birthplace of artist Henri de Toulouse-Lautrec, and the museum dedicated to his works is worth many a return visit.

Also in the southwest is Montpelier, known for cultural life, which is related to its universities. Smaller towns and villages include the Spanish-toned Perpignan and the tiny fishing village of Collioure.

The southwest is not far from the Biarritz beaches. In this area, you can enjoy the fresh fish, particularly anchovies and shrimp. The inland area is famous for *cassoulet*, the legendary dish made with beans and combinations of duck, pork, lamb, or sausage.

Lower altitudes in the southwest have mild winters and torrid summers. Mountain areas are colder, of course.

> *Where we live, the weather changes in strange ways.*
> *We have four seasons, sometimes all in the same month. But even*
> *if the weather's bad here, the Pyrénées form a weather barrier;*
> *we can nip on over to Spain. So we do it a lot.*
>
> —Cary, Pau

The Center

Loire Valley

A few hours' drive from Paris lies the central *Val de Loire* named after France's longest river. The area also encompasses the Cher, the Indre, the Loir (this version drops the *e* on the end), and numerous smaller rivers, in addition to the Loire.

Unlike the dramatic Breton cliffs or the golden Provençal hills, this is a country of gently rolling terrain covered with vineyards and a patchwork of bright yellow fields that, depending on the season are likely to be covered with either sunflowers or *colza*, the yellow rapeseed, which France uses as a form of fuel. The area is *tranquille*. Sedate wine roads and gentle hills make the area excellent for biking and walking. With numerous forests, hunting is also a popular activity in the Loire Valley.

The Loire is the heartland of France in more ways than its location. The spoken French is said to be among the purest in France. The Loire Valley is known as the Garden of France, where farming and vineyards are a way of life. Outside of the famous *châteaux*, such as Chenonceau, Chaumont, and Chambord, the tour buses continue to pass, and people who live here maintain a quiet pace.

Living in the Loire affords the resident opportunity to encounter the *vrai* France, while also remaining close enough to Paris for the occasional weekend or even day trip. The fast train TGV travels from Tours or Le Mans directly to Paris (and to Roissy airport north of the city) in a little less than an hour.

The Loire is not packed wall-to-wall with English speakers as is Provence or the Côte d'Azur, which will encourage you to learn French more quickly. However, there are enough English speakers that you won't lack for an occasional break from speaking French.

Popular wisdom claims that the Loire River marks the change from a northern European climate to a more southerly one. This may be true, but the area won't be confused with the Riviera. Winters are often gloomy, for the most part, with a dark cover of clouds and drizzle. You won't be shoveling snow though; a light dusting of the white stuff occurs just once or twice a year, and even that melts within a few hours.

Burgundy

The Rhône Valley is a peaceful region of rolling hills covered with the vines that create the Burgundy red wines that are delicious to drink and popular in wine-based sauces. Gently competing with the vineyards are yellow fields of mustard. Does the word *Dijon* ring a bell? It's one of this region's main cities.

Bucolic, yes. But Burgundy's pristine fields and forests are located just two hours from Paris on a good *autoroute*. Once in Burgundy, it's easy to get around with good roads. You'll want to use them to explore the villages. Better yet, try biking on quiet and flat country roads or along the numerous canals.

Not only is Burgundy convenient to Paris (one-and-a-half hours by TGV), it's only a hop, skip, and a jump to Switzerland, Italy, and the Mediterranean.

The climate is mild in Burgundy. Though not exactly warm in January, temperatures usually stay above freezing, so you'll avoid shoveling snow in winter. Summers are temperate, ranging from the high 70s to the low 80s.

THE NORTHWEST

Normandy

Green flowing hills, apple trees, World War II monuments, and wharves packed with fresh fish capture the essence of things Norman. Here, where the Americans (and Brits and Canadians, lest we forget) came ashore in WWII to free the French, people still haven't forgotten. Somehow the welcome here always seems warmer for Americans than anywhere else I've traveled in France.

Most of the towns in Normandy suffered greatly in World War II bombing but have been beautifully rebuilt. The countryside is endlessly green, dotted by the black and white of lumbering cows and divided by hedges that were the bane of soldiers.

Ports, such as Dinard and Hornfleur, capture the traditional sea-faring feeling of the Norman coast. Cherbourg puts you within ferry-range of Britain. And Caen is the big busy city that charms with its pedestrian areas and fine restaurants. The TGV from Paris takes just over an hour to get to Rouen, bringing the area within easy striking distance.

Real estate in Normandy offers you choices of historic homes to fix up or new homes. All seem especially reasonable in price. Perhaps it's due to the supply and demand factor—a large supply of cold, cloudy weather and little demand compared to other areas of France. However the people are warmhearted, it's close to Paris when an infusion of excitement is in order, and if you don't mind gloomy weather, it can be a lovely place to live.

Brittany

In the northwest corner of France, the closest area to Great Britain (for which it is named) is Brittany. Celtic influences remain in the festivals and fascinating regional costumes, including the high, starched headdresses that look as though they'd sail away in the Atlantic breeze. Fortunately for the women, these are only worn during special festivals, not in daily life.

Craggy cliffs line the sea, which rises and falls dramatically. Prehistoric monuments, such as Carnac, add to the mystical flavor of the area with its awe-inspiring stone monoliths.

You'll be eating more crepes than usual here, those thin pancakes filled with ham or cheese or fruit. You'll enjoy the freshest Atlantic seafood imaginable. Walk along the piers when the catch is in and pick the fresh Atlantic seafood directly from the boats. Mussels (*moules*) and oysters (*huîtres*) will be heaped along the wharves in huge bins—unrefrigerated even in summer. This shocked me until I realized that with seafood this fresh, it hardly matters, since it's eaten within a few hours of being taken from the waters.

If you take your meal in a restaurant, it's no surprise that the favorite menu is *moules/frites*, mussels with french fries. Try mussels plain, mussels with cream, mussels with tomatoes, and mussels with garlic. Even if you think you don't like mussels, try them in Brittany. The fresh perfection is the only way to initiate yourself and may make you a believer. I speak from experience. I would not touch those sleek black crescents until my husband insisted I try one of his at dinner. I quickly ordered my own bowl heaped with the little critters and have been consuming them with pleasure throughout France ever since.

The climate is "brrrr" Atlantic where the fog and rain first rolls in, which doesn't make Brittany tops on the expatriate list. But this is a benefit in escaping the English-speaking hordes or high costs of the southern areas.

> *Haute-Savoie is one of the loveliest areas of France.*
> *This is confirmed by the fact that it is a favorite*
> *in-country tourist location for the French themselves.*
> —Dorothy, Haute-Savoie

THE NORTHEAST

Alsace

Is it really France, or is it Germany? Alsace has been a Ping-Pong ball between the two countries. It's French these days but the culture is definitely Germanic. Most of the residents speak both French and German, the latter due not only to their forebears but also to the hordes of German tourists. The medieval and Renaissance architecture includes wonderful half-timbered houses. The city of Strasbourg showcases them in the old town where dark timbers contrast with miles of colorful flower boxes on the houses lining the paths that follow canals and pedestrian bridges. Strasbourg is much more than a picturesque idyll. It is one of the most cosmopolitan European cities and the seat of the Council of Europe and European Parliament, with luxury hotels and convention centers, sophisticated transportation, and elegant stores.

The food here is hardier than anywhere else in France, featuring Germanic specialties like *Sauerbraten* or *Flammekuche,* a pizza-like concoction topped with caramelized onions, bits of ham, and rich *crème fraîche.* The French accent shows in the merging of cuisine; for example, the traditional German-style *Sauerbraten* comes with a French-style cream sauce.

If you like white wine, you'll enjoy Alsace, where the *Route de Vin* links wine villages that produce the crisp Riesling and Gewürztraminer.

Alsace is not an area for beach bums, as it is located in the Vosges mountains, which are beautifully forested. The countryside is beautiful for hiking, but be prepared for the northern European climate of snowy winters and moderate summers.

WAIT, THERE'S MORE!

No one can possibly sum up the tremendous variety to be encountered in France. The above is just a smattering of the more popular regions; within each region lie countless special spots just waiting to be discovered. Those areas may not be so well known, but they are just as beautiful—or more so, if you want to uncover your own spot.

This brings to mind Margot, who lives in the Drôme Provençale, an area that appears to be too far off-the-beaten-path for her dream of running a B&B—except that the path is actually on a route from France to Geneva in Switzerland.

Once you've chosen a general area of the country, focus in on the particular town, village, or farm that best suits your personality and plans.

Study areas and determine what is most important to you. You may even be surprised and fall in love with a locale quite unexpectedly, as we did. We settled in one place, intending to use it only temporarily, then discovered a way of life that suited us and stayed.

Whether the choice is studied or serendipitous, base it on your own innate needs and desires; then enjoy.

3
The Paper Trail

IT IS NOT THE GOING OUT OF PORT, BUT THE COMING IN,
THAT DETERMINES THE SUCCESS OF A VOYAGE.
—Henry Ward Beecher, *Proverbs from Plymouth Pulpit* (1887)

Bureaucracy is a boring word, implying mountains of paperwork, incomprehensible fees, and long waits while a stranger determines your fate. Will you be allowed to live in France? Or will you be condemned to spending three months or less within its borders?

Consider yourself a Hercule Poirot-to-be and the process of applying for passports, visas, and work permits a mystery to be solved. Gather the clues piece-by-tedious-piece, then properly position them so they make your case to the powers-that-be. It requires concentration on your part, but if you apply yourself diligently, you will be amply rewarded with the right to settle happily—and legally—into your new life in France.

START WITH A PASSPORT

If your stay in France will be three months or less, you'll only need a passport. Otherwise, non-European Union visitors (that's you if you're American) are required to have a long-stay visa (*visa de long séjour*) in order to stay in France more than three months.

To apply for the visa, you must first have the passport. If you don't already have one, get an application at designated post offices (even if yours isn't designated, they can tell you which local offices are), courthouses, or over the Internet. When you apply, you must show proof of citizenship, including your original (not a copy) birth certificate. You'll also need two passport photos, which are two by two inches in size taken against a light background. Don't try for dramatic shadowed or slim-the-face poses. I tried that and simply got sent back to do the straight mug shot.

Take the completed application, supporting documents, and photos to the passport agency. They will not immediately give you a passport. Instead, they'll send the paperwork to one of the main U.S. Passport Agencies, located in Boston, Chicago, Honolulu, Houston, Los Angeles, Miami, New Orleans, New York, Philadelphia, San Francisco, Seattle, Stamford, or Washington, D.C. The appropriate agency will issue the passport.

Passports cost $65 for a new application. They're valid for ten years, provided the applicant is at least eighteen years old. Children need their own passports, even infants. A child younger than eighteen gets a five-year passport for $40. The child's passport can't be renewed, as can an adult's, but must be reapplied for. Children from thirteen to eighteen must apply for passports in person, but legal guardians can apply for younger children.

If you have a passport already, check the expiration date and renew it if it will expire within six months. You can renew with a DSP-83 mail-in form, which is available at the same places as original passport applications. Just mail in your old passport, two recent passport photos, and a check or money order for a fee, currently $55.

Allow time to apply to receive a passport, because the process can take three to five weeks, depending on the time of year. Spring and summer are particularly busy times.

Tracking Down a Visa

As mentioned, you must have the passport before applying for a visa, and the visa takes even more time to receive than a passport. A visa is not provided by the U.S. government, but is an endorsement placed in your passport by the French government, which permits you to visit for the specified period of time. The process is more time-consuming than for a passport, because the French consulate in the United States must send your paperwork to France for approval.

If you will be staying longer than three months, France requires that you not only apply for, but have the French visa in hand *before* leaving the United States. You cannot apply for a visa from overseas. Nor can you pick it up there. If you marry a handsome Frenchman (or charming Frenchwoman) you still need a visa (*pour mariage*) before arriving in France. Start the process at least three months in advance to ensure you're not panicked at the last minute, with plane tickets in hand but left at the gate.

To apply for a visa, call the nearest French embassy or consulate and request the visa forms. You'll fill out eight copies of each and will need passport-style photos for each of the eight. As with passports, the regulations require that photos be taken against a plain, light-colored background, and you must face forward.

The paperwork required for a visa includes:

- A valid passport
- A birth certificate
- Passport photos
- Proof of French residence (This can be a lease, electric bill, or a *certificat d'hébergement*.)
- Proof of financial resources (bank statements or stock reports, enough to prove that you can live without the French dole)
- Health insurance (Proof of expatriate insurance, or that your U.S. provider will cover you sufficiently overseas)
- Marriage or divorce certificate
- Affidavit of good conduct from your stateside police.

> *One of my husband's accounting clerks, who's French,*
> *went with us [to apply for a residence permit]. If it weren't for her,*
> *we'd still be stumbling around. The clerks made each of us take a ticket,*
> *though we were all there for the same thing. Then the clerks spent 20 minutes*
> *talking on a coffee break, while we sat and watched!*
> —Amanda, Paris

Sticky Points and How to Solve Them

Two of the above visa requirements are tricky. First, you must have proof of permanent accommodations in France. A hotel doesn't suffice. But if you're not there, you may not yet have a permanent address. It's the old Catch-22 similar to "I need experience, but how do I get it if I can't get the job without experience?"

If you're moving for a job, then you may have accommodations provided by your employer, which will solve the problem. But if you're simply moving to France for sabbatical or retirement, you may be stymied. We solved the problem with the help of a friend in France, who very nicely made the requisite trip to her local *mairie* for *certificat d'hébergement* forms. These forms say that you'll be staying with that person when you arrive in France. If you know anyone already living in France; this is a simple way of meeting the lodging requirement. Don't worry; there's no regulation that says you must actually live with the friend once you arrive.

The second sticky point is the one requiring medical coverage. You must prove that you have adequate insurance to protect you in France. Many American insurance companies won't cover you overseas, but if your coverage will, then copy the appropriate paperwork. You may, as we did, have to get a letter to this fact, signed by a representative of the company. In any case, this comes in handy if you need to use the benefits and the company suddenly develops amnesia and claims that it doesn't cover you in France. In most cases, if you live in France your U.S. coverage won't protect you. Neither will Medicare, so make arrangements for other coverage. Expatriate policies are available. See chapter 21, "A Toast to Your Health," for more details.

> *The visa's really no problem, but if you come to work, it's different.*
> *It took us over a year to get the proper papers with the help of a French friend.*
> —Sara, Vernoux

SPECIAL CASES AND WORK PERMITS

Employees or students need different paperwork. Getting a work permit requires giving up your firstborn, because France's unemployment rate is typically in the double-digits. If you are being transferred with your job or, miracle of miracles, have found employment before moving, your employer will know the best way to go about getting the necessary paperwork accomplished. If you're on your own, the best solution, since cases differ, is simply to inquire at the nearest French consulate, follow their instructions, and pray to the patron saint of impossible cases. For more discussion of work permits, see chapter 19.

RESIDENCE PERMITS

To live in France longer than ninety days in a row you must have a residence permit (*carte de séjour*). First you must have the previously mentioned long-stay visa (*visa de long séjour*). Take this to the nearest town hall (*mairie*) when you first arrive at your new "home" in France and request the *carte de séjour.*

You'll need the same paperwork you used to get the visa. This is totally illogical, because you obviously provided all that paperwork originally or you wouldn't have the visa. I asked about this but never got any answer, other than "that's just the way it is"; so keep all the original paperwork together in a file and take it with you to the *mairie.*

Documents written in English must be translated by an official translator. We tried to get around this by translating our own. Right, and pigs can fly. The translator must be certified. When someone tells you that you need a translation that's *agrée*, that's what they mean. Don't have the translations done before you know which ones they'll want. It's costly, so you might as well wait and let the officials tell you which papers are needed. To find a translator who's *agrée*, ask the *mairie*, the consulate, or see the local yellow pages.

You'll eventually need to pass a physical at your expense, from an approved physician. The letter you receive in France concerning this physical will tell you when and where to report, though you can change the date if it's not convenient for you. Some people have had this physical done before leaving the States, but they report that the physician must be from the French consulate's approved list.

With today's open European borders, it's difficult to prove where you are and whether you're really in France for three months—or across the border in Spain. In any case, your total stay in France can't extend officially beyond 90 days in a row, or six months (180 days) for the entire year, unless you have a residence permit.

TYPES OF RESIDENCE PERMITS

Residence permits come in different flavors, depending on whether you're a visitor, employee, spouse, family member, or student.

The *carte de séjour temporaire* is a temporary residence permit. The temporary residence permit applies to EU and non-EU (European Union) passport holders. It's valid up to one year, and it must be renewed.

The *carte de résidence* is the ten-year residence permit, which you can apply for after you've lived in France for three years.

The bureaucracy is time-consuming and seems to be a pain in the neck, especially when you'd rather be visiting a local art gallery or biking the vineyards, but it's one way to settle in and meet people. You might luck out and, after the repeated visits required to the *mairie*, make your first friends. In our case, the wife of a local vintner worked at the *mairie* where we applied and we've gotten special tastings ever since!

If you ever get exhausted by the bureaucracy, just consider it a good excuse to treat yourself to a leisurely French dinner and remind yourself why you're here.

> *Finding your way within the maze of French bureaucracy*
> *and battling the language difference is an enervating, exciting,*
> *and often exhausting process that forces one to be creative. It was necessary*
> *to totally recreate myself, draw on talents I had that weren't immediately*
> *apparent, and start a new life with a different point of view.*
> —Adrian, Paris

CUSTOMS ON ARRIVAL

Your first step on French soil will most likely be at one of the international airports. Most of the U.S. flights go to Paris, though if you're heading south, you may choose to go through Nice or Marseilles. The arrival procedure is basically the same wherever you land, so let's just assume that you'll arrive in Paris.

There are two airports serving Paris: Charles de Gaulle/Roissy and Orly. Charles de Gaulle/Roissy is about forty-five minutes (depending on traffic) northeast of central Paris. Orly is about a half an hour southwest.

Your first official greeters to France will be the customs officials. Unless you're wearing a fake mustache, a trenchcoat bulging with automatic weapons, and toting three suitcases of cocaine, the procedure is usually quick and painless.

Two lines form, one for people holding EU (European Union) passports, the other for anyone else. That's you. You will be requested to show your passport and customs form. Follow the crowds to collect your baggage and you've arrived.

Both Roissy and Orly airports are connected by train and *Métro* to Paris. Roissy also offers the high-speed TGV train directly to many cities outside Paris. Since you're likely to have more baggage than the average tourist if you're moving to France, be sure to reserve a rental car before leaving the States. It's usually cheaper if you reserve from there. Rentals are an expensive way to get around, however; keep yours just until you're at your final France destination and have the time to find a good used car.

Knowing the law, as well as what you want, is very important.
French civil servants adore rules, and they have millions of them.
They don't understand them, but won't admit it, so they make up their
own as they go along.... Remember this when being passed on to another
civil servant, because you will be faced with yet another set of requirements
for which you have arrived unprepared. (First they look to see what papers
you do have, then they add something unforeseen to the list.)
—Margo, Rémuzat, Drôme Provençale

LIFESTYLES: DRAWING ON LIFE IN PROVENCE

If the number of books, paintings, and photographs devoted to the region are any indication, Provence is the most famous area of France. This land of rosemary, lavender, honey, and olives has produced a cult of adoring fans.

Artists like Jill Steenhuis claim that the area's golden glow has a magnetic attraction. The soft ocher light of the sun buries itself into the honey-colored rock. Even the houses pulse with it, since they're made of the same stone, topped with red tile roofs. Fields of purple lavender are the ideal complement to the golden hues, as though painted from an artist's palette.

Near Aix-en-Provence, Cézanne found his muse in the unique shape of Mont-Sainte-Victoire. So did Jill. She followed in Cézanne's footsteps, studying the mountain at an artist's atelier in nearby Le Tholenet. "I came to do a six-week summer program, then was supposed to go back to be a stockbroker...never in my wildest dreams would I have left my roots, but destiny had it worked out otherwise."

She couldn't make herself leave. (Well, meeting her *prince charmant*, Serge, did encourage the process.) Now she lives in an old French *"mas"* or farmhouse with husband and three Franco-American sons. She trundles her palette to the surrounding fields, often rising at five in the morning to capture the early light. The results are increasing numbers of exhibitions, especially back in the United States, where she returns to see family and friends. "I do what I love to do the most and it has become a way of life."

If you were to paint in Provence, what would you do as a respite from all this stress? Take a picnic to Mont-Sainte-Victoire park and watch hang gliders soar like wildly colored butterflies from the peak above. Or try your hand at *pétanque*, the slow-paced game played in squares throughout Provence. Games are interrupted civilly from time to time for a sip of the licorice-flavored liqueur, pastis.

Enjoy Provençale meals that are Mediterranean in character and include the freshest of produce from local farms. Try roast lamb with garlic, melons from Cavaillon, olives, and tapenade, a crushed olive spread that's served on fresh slices of baguette.

The pace is slow here, and that's pleasant (unless it's the slowness of traffic on the summer-crowded routes to the sea and vacation homes). If you're not going anywhere, just sit back and watch the olive trees grow.

You too might reflect, as Jill does, "Somehow, all the pieces came together...you wonder why you're so lucky."

4
Speaking Your Mind

IN PARIS, THEY SIMPLY STARED WHEN I SPOKE TO THEM IN FRENCH;
I NEVER DID SUCCEED IN MAKING THOSE IDIOTS
UNDERSTAND THEIR OWN LANGUAGE.
—Mark Twain

"Do you speak French?" people ask in awe when they learn you live in France. We Americans, being leagues across the pond from Europe, consider it a minor miracle to speak another language.

Before you let fear of the French language spoil any dreams you may have of living in France, consider that learning French is not the impassable mountain most people assume. If worse comes to worse, some English-speaking people here hardly speak it at all and still manage. English is the most popular second language in Europe. It's spoken widely in Paris and the most popular areas. One American woman in the heavily touristed area of Provence brags that she's lived in France sixteen years and still can't speak French. I'm sure she's exaggerating. At least I hope so.

Just because some people live here without speaking French, don't emulate them. If you plan to live in France, you'll be better served—both figuratively and literally—if you can speak the language. This is true in most countries and even more so in France, where the people take special pride in their language.

French has a centuries-long history as the language of culture and diplomacy. These days it's the official language of the United Nations, UNESCO, the International Committee for the Olympic Games, the International Monetary Fund, and the International Red Cross, among others.

As a first or second language, it's spoken by people in Europe, the Orient, Africa, and the Caribbean—in fact, French is spoken in countries spread across all continents. Although English is widely studied in France, it's not the language of daily life. If you want to live in France, learning French should be your first goal.

> *Knowing French expands your experience. You won't spend an entire day hiking in the mountains, like we just did with a [French] friend, then come back while he slowly cooks a whole leg of lamb. If you didn't speak the language, you'd never have a day like that.*
> —Melanie, Pau

A PEP TALK À LA FRANÇAISE

Knowing French heightens the experience and understanding of the country. You can participate fully in life in France only if you can be a part of it, and that takes communication.

Speaking French removes barriers to understanding the country and its people. Think of the misunderstandings that arise due to miscommunication even when you're speaking your native tongue. Just imagine when you don't understand the language at all!

Understanding and speaking French enables you to broaden your range of social contacts from other English speakers to the French community. As a sideline, you'll meet other internationals as well. Those living in France will most likely speak the language, and you'll hear French spoken with German, Italian, Portuguese, Spanish, and Dutch accents. The world is your *huître*.

Speaking French enables you to participate in your favorite arts, sports, and hobbies without limiting yourself to courses and clubs designed for English speakers. This is particularly helpful if you choose to live outside of Paris or tourist-populated areas.

If you're living in France, you are conveniently located for travel in Western Europe. Knowing French will help you travel confidently. Even if you don't speak Italian and German, Portuguese and Spanish, adding French to your repertoire doubles your chances of understanding and being understood by someone in those countries. When we missed a train at ten o'clock at night in Florence and needed to find the next one quickly, we couldn't find anyone who spoke English, but one of the Italian reservation clerks did speak French.

*My daughter was only eight when we moved here
five years ago, and she's perfectly fluent in French—
even prefers to read in it—while I'm still struggling.*
—Adrian, Paris

Learning as Child's Play

No one will tell you that learning French is simple—though it *is* child's play. Children pick up language skills so adroitly that it puts us adults to shame. Yes, you'll feel intimidated when you first start learning French. You don't hear the ends of the words, the syllables all run together, and you have no idea how to get your tongue around those strange "ooh" and "rrrr" sounds. *Don't* use difficulty as an excuse to put off learning. Start like a child with simple language. Then play at building the blocks you'll need, with the blocks being one word, one grammar rule, one proper pronunciation at a time.

Don't set your goals too high. You're not expected to know French perfectly, just enough to manage on a daily basis. You'll gradually improve.

Do work at it. My husband is living proof of the potential for even the most elementary students to achieve, if not fluency, at least proficiency in daily communication. He began at ground zero, knowing just one phrase that served him well on our initial vacations here: *"Je voudrais du vin, s'il vous plaît."* The positive reinforcement occurred when he got the requested glass of wine.

He's dedicated to improving and has been studying diligently. Finally, I heard him converse on the phone; haltingly, sure, but communicating nonetheless. That's all you need and the rest will come eventually.

LE BON MOT: Language Skills

Cours . . . . Course
Langue maternelle . . Native tongue
Professeur . . . . Teacher
Tutoyer . . . . To use, the familiar "tu"
Vouvoyer . . . . To use the formal "vous"

Begin with the Basics

Start learning French before you arrive in France. Learn the general structure and pronunciation rules, plus the basic elements of grammar and whatever vocabulary you can muster. Once you live in France, the opportunities for learning expand exponentially, but you'll need that basic understanding to take advantage of it.

Concentrate on survival words first. These include the basic polite phrases for hello, please, thank you, and you're welcome. Learn numbers and the alphabet in French. The former are essential for phone calls and shopping, addresses and banking. The alphabet helps pronunciation and enables you to spell your name for reservations or find out the correct spelling of the street you're looking for.

Speaking of streets, learn directional words, such as left, right, straight ahead...and where's the bathroom?

Don't panic when you see the numerous verb tenses that are possible in French. Know that they exist but concentrate on learning one—the present tense—and later you can expand to past and future. Wait to acquire the more erudite tenses, such as imperfect and subjunctive, once you've got the basics down pat.

French has two forms of verbs for "you," the formal *"vous"* and the familiar *"tu."* Aside from knowing that the familiar form exists, ignore it. As a rank beginner, practice only the *"vous"* form. It simplifies the learning, and you can't go wrong with it.

I still recall that once on a train, two Frenchmen in front of me almost came to blows. The major complaint the one man had, which he repeated in fury three times to the conductor, was not that the other man had called him an idiot, but that the man had dared to use the familiar *"tu"* to him!

> You have to ante into the poker game and learn the language.
> You're not interesting to your [French] friends when learning,
> because you're like a two- or four-year-old. But it's tough for adults,
> because they don't want to be a child again.
> —Cary, Pau

FORMAL OR INFORMAL STUDY?

Some people study French in schools or with tutors. Others prefer to take control of their own learning with tapes, CDs, and books. The fact is, different techniques emphasize different skills, and you need them all at different times in the learning process.

When you first study French, it helps to have a teacher, either in a class or in individual lessons. The teacher can start you off on the right *pied* by explaining rules of grammar and pronunciation that you might not get from tapes or a book. And a teacher provides practice in conversation that no other method will provide.

You can use many other means to learn French as well. Listening to television and radio helps your comprehension—and your pronunciation if you repeat new words to yourself. Reading will increase your vocabulary as you learn words in context. A good grammar textbook will teach you the rules and remind you of ones you forget. Regular conversations with neighbors and friends will improve your speaking skills.

Steve speaks French to one man in town, who always responds in English. Finally he had to put his foot down and said he needed to practice his French!
—Pam, Le Mans

Faux Amis

False friends are *faux amis*. Nope, these aren't people who snub you, but rather words in French that are especially troublesome, because they look like an English word, but mean something entirely different. There are numerous *faux amis*, but here are a few common examples.

Actuel /Actualités	*Actuel* is an event occurring at the present moment, with *actualités* being the television news. Do not use this the way Americans use "actual." That's *vrai*.
Apologie	Praise. If you spill wine it's "*mes excuses*."
Assistance/assister	Audience or to attend. Not "help." For that, use *aide* or the verb *aider*.
Caméra	Motion picture camera. What tourists wear around their necks is called an *appareil photo*.
Commander	This is how you'll order a cake or a special cut of meat. To issue a command in stronger fashion is *ordonner*.
Demander	To ask, not the harsher English "demand." For months I felt positively rude whenever I "demanded" anything of friends.
Interprète	Actor or actress, not interpreter.
Raisin	Grape. The dried up, English-language raisin is a *raisin sec*.
Prune	Plum. A prune is a *pruneau* in French.

Formal Language Studies

Preferably you'll start learning French before arriving in France. You'll find courses in adult education at community schools, college night courses, language schools, such as Berlitz and Inlingua, and Alliance Française groups.

When choosing a learning setting, consider your level of French, the cost, and the time you have available. Do you prefer to learn in a classroom situation or would you prefer one-on-one training or self-study? For better pronunciation, make sure that you are studying with someone whose native tongue (*langue maternelle*) is French.

In France, you'll discover that large cities, especially Paris, offer dozens of language schools and training centers and hundreds of tutors. Get-togethers are held to enable foreigners to practice the art of conversation. Here are a few possibilities:

Accord. This language school specializes in French courses for adults and offers courses at all levels. Year-round classes, summer, and evening courses are offered along with specialized courses, such as a theater workshop, business French, and an arts program for students developing dance, painting, music, sculpture, or architecture works in conjunction with Wells College. Contact: Accord, 14 boulevard Poissonnière, 75009 Paris; telephone 01 55 33 52 33; fax 01 55 33 52 34; e-mail: *accordel@easynet.fr*; website: *http://www.accord-langues.com/*.

L'Alliance Française. Founded in 1883, *l'Alliance Française* promotes the French language and culture throughout the world. The group operates in more than 130 countries, including the United States. Not just a language school, this is like a club for francophiles. As a member or student, you can borrow books from their library and participate in various cultural events.

Classes are held for beginning to advanced students, including discussions of French history and culture. Their methods are sound, the people are friendly, and it has a solid reputation.

In the United States, contact *Alliance Française*, 2142 Wyoming Avenue NW, Washington, DC 20008; telephone: (202) 234-7911.

In France, contact *Alliance Française de Paris*, 101, boulevard Raspail, 75270 Paris, Cedex 06; telephone: 01 45 44 38 28; fax: 01 45 44 89 42; e-mail: *info@alliancefrancaise.fr*; website: *http://www.alliancefrancaise.fr*.

Berlitz. The company has more than 320 language schools in 36 countries worldwide, with five locations in or near Paris and eleven in the French provinces. The school emphasizes a natural-learning system and covers elementary through advanced levels in group, individual, computer, or telephone courses. Additional services include cross-cultural studies, conversation groups, translation, and business services, such as editing. Contact Berlitz Champs-Elysées, 35, avenue Franklin D. Roosevelt, 75008 Paris; telephone: 01 40 74 00 17; fax 01 45 61 49 79; website: *http://www.berlitz.com/*.

Business Talk France. Focuses on business French at all levels with individual or small group lessons, telephone courses, and office lessons. Contact Business Talk France, 134, boulevard Haussmann, 75008 Paris; telephone 01 49 53 91 83; fax 01 45 62 13 11; e-mail: *btf@clubinternet.fr*.

Cours de Langue et Civilisation Française de la Sorbonne. Offers academic French language and civilization courses associated with one of the more prestigious names in French education, the Sorbonne. Courses are held for all levels, beginner to advanced; except for a few three-week sessions in the summer, these are rigorous academic courses. As might be expected, this school caters to teachers and serious students.

Contact Cours de Langue et Civilisation Française de la Sorbonne, 47, rue des Ecoles, 75005 Paris; telephone 01 40 46 22 11, extensions 2664 and 2675; fax 01 40 46 32 29; e-mail: *ccfs@paris4.sorbonne.fr*; website: *http://www.fle.fr/sorbonne.*

L'Institut Catholique de Paris. A private Catholic university, *la Catho* offers courses to the general public in language and cultural studies, though most students come for a year or a summer. Courses offered include language classes for beginners to advanced, plus cultural courses in art, cinema, and media. Contact l'Institut Catholique de Paris, 21, rue d'Assas, 75270 Paris Cedex 06; telephone: 01 44 39 52 68; fax: 01 44 39 52 09.

Université Aix-Marseille III. This school offers two semester-long courses (October to February, or February to May) or intensive summer sessions of three to four weeks in length. Courses in all levels. Contact Institut d'Études Françaises pour Étudiants Étrangers, 23, rue Gaston-de-Soporta, 13625 Aix-en-Provence, Cedex. Telephone: 04 42 21 70 90; fax: 04 42 23 02 64.

Tutors

A tutor can provide one-on-one training, but check the credentials of the person to make sure they have teaching skills. Prices will range based on professionalism from about 50 or 60 francs an hour in the countryside to 100 francs an hour or more in the city.

For tutors, see the advertisements in the various English-language papers in Paris, including *France-USA Contacts,* which has acres of listings, as does the *Paris Free Voice.* Notice boards at the American Church and American Library are other sources.

You may even find someone who wants to trade French lessons for English lessons, which will drastically cut the cost. Of course, if you're both amateurs at teaching language, this type of unstructured learning can turn into unlearning. So be prepared with a plan for your sessions before your "meetings" dissolve into aimless chitchat.

Discussion Groups

An extension of the one-on-one language exchange mentioned above is the discussion group. These are becoming popular forums for people to practice French and/or English. Such groups meet socially in order to have a place in which to speak the language. Some are chaired by a language teacher. Others are more informal.

Parler Parlor is open to French people who want to learn English and English speakers learning French. Half the meeting is held in each language. The meetings are held at Berlitz France in Paris, though the school does not coordinate the meetings. For information contact Berlitz at 01 40 27 97 59; e-mail: *leeds@wfi.fr*; website: *http://www.parlerparlor.com*.

Konversando is a language exchange group between English, French, Spanish, German, and Italian speakers. The group meets at 8 bis, Cité Trévise 75009; telephone: 01 47 70 21 64.

For other groups, of which there are dozens, check the *Paris Free Voice* or *France-USA Contacts* (*FUSAC*) classified listings for professional groups or individuals who would like to share conversation.

> *Our discussion group combines fluent French speakers and beginners,*
> *which doesn't sound like it would work; but it's great, because beginners*
> *alone wouldn't be able to hold much conversation. This way they can listen,*
> *and the more fluent people make an effort to draw them out.*
>
> —Adrian, Paris

DAILY IMPROVEMENTS

When you arrive in France, the language will sound so different, you'll wonder what it is you actually began learning in the United States. Words have a rhythm and emphasis that you'll gradually become accustomed to hearing. You'll start improving your comprehension, learning new idioms, and perfecting your pronunciation, as your ear picks up the nuances.

This daily immersion in speaking French is why your skills will grow by leaps and bounds once you live in France. Best of all, you can hasten the process in these painless ways.

Be a Couch Pomme de Terre

Watching television is not why you moved to France, I agree. But on cold, dark nights, flip through the dial to find shows you're interested in or that match your learning level. In the early morning, you can watch cartoons; because they are designed for children, they are relatively simple in language. The only negative is that the childish voices may actually make the words more difficult to understand.

French news announcers and politicians speak slowly and thoughtfully, so the news shows are good programs to watch, unless they're talking about specific and complicated political agendas. Game shows, especially the ones that play on words, can be fun ways to learn.

Your favorite programs from the states may be showing, dubbed into French. You can follow those well, since you're already familiar with the characters and basic storyline.

French movies on the television channels France One, Two, and Three are often subtitled for the deaf, an option you can access through your remote control by activating TeleText and entering 8-8-8. This is a wonderful option for learning French, since the words show on the screen as they're spoken. *Voila!* You're learning pronunciation. (Don't be ashamed of muttering words out loud for pronunciation practice.)

If one program is too difficult, try another one. Some programs that are translated from English are easier to follow than others. French takes more words than English, and some translators cram in the words so that the voice-over becomes rushed. In other programs, the translators capture the gist of it but at a normal pace.

Radio

Many people recommend listening to the radio. Certainly it will provide an immersion in the language and help you gain a feel for the rhythm. Other than that, I haven't found this to be especially helpful until you reach an advanced level of comprehension, because radio, unlike television, provides no visual clues.

We sometimes turn on the car radio for practice on trips, though a word of warning: If you're concentrating on understanding the radio announcer, you may take your concentration off the wheel, which is definitely not recommended around French drivers!

Videocassettes

If you have access to a VCR (*magnetoscope*), videos can help your French comprehension, since you can—you can, you can, you can—play them back, if you don't understand the first time.

If you're interested in a sport or hobby, pick out a video on that subject. It's a handy way to learn the technical terms involved.

Newspapers, Magazines, and Books

Join the local library and begin reading children's books, if you need to. You might also enjoy the adult comic books that are very popular in France. They're called *bandes dessinées*. The comic strips for adults are definitely adult in topic and theme, often with the same sex and violence you might see in an R-rated film; so don't give them to a six-year-old!

Sale Flyers and Catalogs

Hmmm, another boring old flyer, you say? Not when you're trying to learn French. Those flyers that stores put out for customers are a great way to learn products, because they put pictures with the product name. You don't even have to know the English word to learn what it is. A *remorque*, I discovered, is an open trailer pulled behind a tractor or car. I know because I saw pictures of them in the ads where I live in the country.

Converse
Make an effort to speak. I know you're shy. Everyone is. But your tongue needs to acclimate itself to those strange syllables. When you're shopping, listen to the people around you and see how they order something. Repeat what they say. (Once I even bought the same four slices of ham and chunk of cheese as the lady in front of me at the deli, just to see if I could say it correctly!)

Talk to Yourself
Okay, so watch when you do this, or you might learn French in the looney bin; but carrying on an imaginary conversation or explaining to yourself what you're doing as you go about daily activities allows you to practice sentence construction and French vocabulary.

Get Involved
Take a class or volunteer or participate in a sport. You'll make French-speaking friends and be forced to speak. Even if you remain mum most of the time, you'll have listening practice in daily life. Besides, being totally at sea provides the motivation to work harder at improving your French.

Make Friends
Informal friendships allow you to learn as you go. As you speak regularly to the same person, you become accustomed to their style of speech. This is a mixed blessing; it will be easier to understand a close friend but you also should adjust to different accents, pacing, and common phrases.

One friend, Marie-France, makes an effort to speak clearly for me, and I've always been able to understand her. She's become an automatic tutor, often finishing my sentences for me when I stop to search for the right words. (If this happens to you, quickly repeat what they just said, so you'll learn from it.) Another friend talked so fast and furiously, that I didn't understand a word. But gradually I became accustomed to her pacing and the way she merges words.

THE BEST DICTIONARY EVER

Invest in a *Harrap's Shorter Dictionnaire*. This bountiful French/English dictionary is thorough, clear, concise, and looks impressive on the coffee table. Use it every day when you see or hear a French word you don't know. Best of all, the 550,000 translations include literal and idiomatic meanings plus sample phrases, so you can see the words used in context.

COPING SKILLS

Speaking on the phone is difficult when you're first learning a language. You don't have all those handy hand signals and facial clues. Is the person mad? Happy? Is he gesticulating wildly toward the exit? The way around this is to use shoe leather at first. Whenever possible, accomplish whatever you can in person. If you need to arrange utility services or ask the *mairie* when to expect garbage pickup, go there in person. Yes, it takes extra time, but it's easier on the nerves, and you'll still get French language practice.

Always say "bonjour." Then switch to English, and hope!
—John, Loire Valley

Be prepared for ups and downs in your language morale. Some days you feel you've made significant progress. The next day you'll feel like a sluggish 78-rpm record in a fast-spinning CD world.

Remember that you are learning in daily life, just by listening. Have patience and pick up a word or phrase here, then another there. Soon you will have accumulated a vocabulary. This is your goal. You can make the process go faster or slower, depending on how active a participant you are in the process.

Most important: don't give up. The day will come when you'll look back and be amazed at your progress.

Ça va arriver. (It'll happen!)

5
Kisses, Handshakes, and Other Shocking Behavior

IN EUROPE, WHERE HUMAN RELATIONS, LIKE CLOTHES,
ARE SUPPOSED TO LAST, ONE'S GOT TO BE WEARABLE.
IN FRANCE ONE HAS TO BE INTERESTING.
—Sybille Bedford, *The Sudden View*

The French are warm, enthusiastic, and friendly to Americans. That's my experience, and I'm sticking to it, because you're more likely to hear countless tourists—whose only experience was the Paris *Métro* at rush hour—claim that all French are arrogant, pushy, and rude.

Not true. Not true. Not true.

You'll know better when you live here. But to start you on the right *pied*, it helps to understand some simple facts about the French culture, so you'll be better prepared to adapt to it.

Learning a culture differs from learning a language; in some ways, it's more difficult, since we tend to expect people to act as we do. Leave preconceptions back in the states and discover the distinctions that make up the French character and way of life. This is part of the experience, and you'll enjoy many of these distinct characteristic. Understanding what to expect before you arrive will greatly ease the transition.

This book covers various aspects of living in France, so cultural distinctions are discussed throughout as they relate to specific topics. However, certain distinctions color the French personality so deeply that they warrant special attention.

Soon you, too, will be able to successfully win French friends and influence the butcher down the *rue* to give you the best cut of meat.

La Politesse

Mom taught you to say "please" and "thank you." Though we Americans don't like to think of ourselves as rude, we're definitely more casual than Europeans when it comes to social niceties.

The French are strongly traditional and certain polite rules of behavior are second nature to them. They're cognizant of whether a person is well behaved or not. The person who behaves well in social situations is *bien elevé*, or well raised, as opposed to *mal elevé*, or badly raised. Of course, this puts a great deal of pressure on the French *mère* to see that her children are never saddled with the latter term. Thus, *la politesse* gathers each new generation under the mother hen's wing.

You, as an American, did not have the advantage of a French mother so French people will make concessions if you forget to say *"bonjour"* once or twice. However, you will definitely make a better impression if you adhere to certain forms.

Bonjour Toujours

In French, the words for "hello" and "always" rhyme. Does this tell you something? *Bonjour* is far more than a simple greeting. Always say it when entering a small shop presided over by an individual. Always say it to the cashier when you pay for your purchases. Always say it at your local library when you check out books. You're safe in saying *bonjour* in any situation when you are dealing face-to-face with a human being.

The only exception is that you are not expected to greet strangers on the street. This one fact alone is undoubtedly why many Americans think the French are unfriendly. Americans in France can bounce hellos off the walls, and chances are there will be no response. It has nothing to do with being friendly. Rather, French people use *bonjour* to recognize someone who's a friend or someone with whom they deal in business. This usually doesn't include strangers who just happen to be standing at the crosswalk with them. French people can't know everyone in the world, and they already say hello to everyone in their part of it hundreds of times a day, so it hardly seems necessary to ask for more.

This particular culture shock works both ways, as I found out years ago in Atlanta when we hosted a French exchange student. We were taking a walk in the neighborhood and passed several different people. We nodded and said hello, but passed without any other words. Each time, Valerie looked at me strangely until finally she blurted out, "Do you know them?"

"No," I said.

"Then why do you say hello?" Hmm, I thought. I don't know. We just do. But not in France.

The cultural differences are worse than the language.
I feel like I'm walking on eggshells all the time.
—Patricia, Paris

Name Games
Americans are quick to reach a first-name basis. In France most people remain *monsieur* or *madame* (or *mademoiselle* for an obviously young, unmarried woman). You'll add the last name (for example, Madame Knorr) if you know it. Even when you become friends and use first names, do not assume that you would then use the familiar *tu* form of "you." Continue to use the formal *vous* until it's obvious, by your friend using *tu* toward you, that you've reached the highest level of friendship.

Save Your Smiles
The French are not against laughter. However, they will not smile just for the sake of smiling. As with saying hello, they do not smile to strangers on the street.

I read somewhere that French politicians try not to smile on camera, because they want to be considered *serieux.* The article noted that Jacques Chirac, as president of France, was so rarely shown with a smile that when a group of French people were shown a photograph of him smiling, no one recognized him. Yes, this particular cultural difference is another reason why the French have that dour reputation.

Making Requests
On a visit back to the States, I was in a shopping center when a woman rushed up, briskly asked directions to Wal-Mart, and scurried away faster than the White Rabbit. I shook my head and wondered why I'd felt uncomfortable with the exchange, then realized that in France this would never happen.

Here, one politely acknowledges any person you come in contact with by first saying *bonjour.* You might add a polite phrase that recognizes that you're intruding, but you really could use their help, something along the lines of "*Excusez-moi de vous déranger*" (Excuse me for bothering you) or simply "*Excusez-moi.*" This opens up the field for the next step, which is to ask your question or make your request.

Kisses
Those cheek-brushing kisses the French are so fond of take some adjustment on the part of Americans. I once had to stop in the middle of leave-taking at a party when a friend laughed in mid-pucker. She proceeded to give me a lesson on *les bisous* (cheek kisses) while the group took off their coats and milled around, trying to decide why *l'américaine* has such a problem with what they consider a simple exercise.

Basically you offer one cheek after the other, usually starting on the right but take the French person's lead to avoid any embarrassing nose-to-nose contact. You don't necessarily kiss the check, just pucker in the general direction. Two kisses are common. Three are appropriate in Paris and between close friends. Four is rare but possible with enthusiasts. Women kiss women. Women kiss men. Men don't kiss other men, they shake hands instead.

Handshakes

Coming and going, even with only two minutes between, the Frenchman's hands exercise themselves in a flurry of shaking. If a man recognizes someone at an adjacent table in a café, he'll trot over and shake hands all around, even with those he doesn't know, just to avoid giving offense. I take an art class in pastels, those all-over-your-hands chalks, and it's a real mess when someone arrives late. Soon we're up to our elbows in dust.

Shhhh

In public, French people talk quietly, so as not to bother other people. Want proof? When you live in France try this test during tourist season. Sit in a café and just listen to people at various tables. Note the difference in decibel levels between the French people and foreigners. Note also that while you're listening to the French, they're listening to you. Always assume that they can understand English. Most French people can understand English much better than they speak it, though often they won't let you know that they understand.

One time a Belgian friend and I had dinner at a local café. We spoke in English to each other, though she could speak fluent French, and did so to the owner of the café. However, in changing from one language to another, she slipped. Turning from me to the owner, she asked about desserts in English. He responded in kind in perfect English. It seems he had lived in the States for years.

I couldn't resist asking why, in all the times I'd been in his restaurant, he'd never spoken to me in English. "You always spoke to me in French" was his reply.

Save yourself embarrassment. Never say anything out loud you wouldn't want everyone nearby to hear.

Le Bon Mot: Six Polite Phrases

Au revoir. . . . . Good-bye
Bonjour. . . . . Hello
Je vous en prie. . . . . You're welcome
Merci. . . . . Thank you
Pardonnez-moi . . . . Excuse me
S'il vous plaît. . . . . Please

Understanding the French Psyche

Aside from the traditional polite forms mentioned, various other elements of the French personality permeate life in France. Understanding them will help you avoid fighting the tide, which will help you adapt to life in France more quickly.

Momentary Pleasure

That wonderful French phrase, *On doit profiter,* means enjoy the moment. Indeed, there are many simple joys to be found in this country, such as a walk on a sunny day, a perfect wine, and a chance conversation with a friend. Profit from this notion. Relax and take time to smell the lavender.

Body Language

The French not only speak a different language, they gesture it. The French person will punctuate words with facial expressions and whirling hands, bringing body language into play much more than an American. Think of it this way: If you adapt to the French style of body language, you'll be getting more exercise to help burn off those croissants.

Another distinction is the European ability to tolerate more closeness in personal space. What feels to the French as normal distance—in an elevator or in a line, for example—occasionally feels crowded to those of us brought up in wide-open spaces.

The Frenchwoman

Women in France are aware of their femininity and won't let a man forget it. They have the same spine as American women, but their posture is different. It's not merely straighter. The French woman has a greater awareness of her body and its positioning. The beauty of it is that this is not done artificially, like a bad actress on stage. It's simply a characteristic bred into little French girls from the cradle. Parisiennes, in particular, seem to take advantage of the grand gestures and small touches that proclaim their femininity.

Does women's lib have an equivalent in France? To a certain extent, it does, in that the modern French woman often works and expects equality in the workplace. However, she will not give up one ounce of her femininity. She still expects to be, as one French career woman told me, "a journalist, a wife, a mother, and a mistress." She said this in front of her husband, so I'm assuming she meant the latter figuratively.

> *I never dared to comment on a woman's appearance in the States,*
> *for all the harassment problems. Here, if I don't comment on my secretary's*
> *new dress, she thinks there's something wrong with her!*
> —Steve, Le Mans

Discussion

The French are proud of their reputation for fine culture and they love discussing every topic to the nth degree, from soccer to movies, from politics to the new sign on the bar down the block. The discussion may even get heated at times. Usually this is simply part of the joy of debate, and a function of the French desire to delve into a subject thoroughly.

If truth be told, you can't get away from discussion in France. The art of conversation is ingrained in the French psyche. Nowhere else is this more true than *à table*. We once took our French teacher to Sunday lunch. After our dinner conversation of two-and-a-half hours, we spent another forty-five minutes after our coats were retrieved, due to a last-minute political discussion with the chef. It would have taken longer but that my husband took our lovely 79-year-old professor gently by the arm—ostensibly to help her.

When you go to the market, don't plan to "just pick something up in five minutes." It'll never happen, unless you wear a disguise, because that's always when you see three friends, all of whom expect the ritual kisses or handshakes and fifteen minutes of polite conversation. It'll drive Type A's nuts at first. The trick is to relax and expect everything to take longer than you may think.

Money

Relationships are more important than money in France. In fact, the French tend to avoid discussing money. One big no-no in France is to ask a mere acquaintance what he does for a living. Since most professions in France have salary structures, this is like asking how much someone makes and is seen as an effort to categorize.

You may be pleasantly surprised that workers in your home—the electrician, for example—may put off providing a bill. He doesn't want to appear to be grasping and practically speaking, he may want to wait until all the work is done first, since the government requires paperwork galore. The good news is, you'll be getting no-interest loans until you get billed.

Food and Wine
Be prepared to talk food, wine, and restaurants in detail. After a few meals in France you'll soon understand why these are popular topics. The wine portion of this goes tenfold if you live in a wine-growing region.

Homes
Hopefully you'll make French friends and be invited to their homes. Be careful about being as casual as you might be in the States. Don't wander around the house or ask to see it. The kitchen, for example, where many Americans virtually entertain, is usually off-limits for formal visitors. The good news is, until you become very close friends, you don't have to help clean up after dinner.

Friendship
The French take friendships seriously. Thus, they develop friendships at a slow pace. Once you're a friend, you'll be expected to participate in the back-and-forth of various social exchanges. This is pleasant, but after the fifth cocktail party in a week, you may yearn for fewer friends. That's the reason why friendships develop slowly.

You'll eventually have a full social calendar, so be selective.

Brotherhood
On the other hand, you don't have to be friends with someone to benefit from the natural French attitude toward taking care of their own. Their own, in this case, can be you, if you become part of the community. There's an amazing amount of flexibility (okay, call it favoritism) in the service a local receives as compared to that of a tourist.

The practical application: Trade with local shops and services. You'll get better baguettes. You'll get told of special deals. And you'll get your electricity or plumbing fixed faster.

Sex and Nudity
The French are not prudish, that's for sure. You'll see bare-breasted women, not just on TV, but at some beaches and parks on a summer day. Sex is considered a normal function of life but violence is not commonly seen as entertainment. Most violent shows are imported via American movies and television serials.

The good news is that men here don't have to waste money on girlie magazines.

Bathroom Humor
Bodily functions are considered normal in France and are not hidden with as much diligence as they are in the States. Which is to say, sometimes they aren't hidden at all. You'll be driving down the road and a man may be standing on the edge of a road, his back to you, who's obviously had too

much French coffee and just can't wait for relief. Though not exactly touted in high society, this type of thing will be seen in France now and then. Even in the bathrooms, it may be share and share alike. The stalls are different, but the central sink can be used by men and women.

The high-tech public toilets seen on Paris streets are very popular. Just as burger stands in the States note the number of sandwiches sold, the signs outside French toilets proudly proclaim "more than 100 million users in Europe." A reasonable two francs provide entrance. Each time a user steps out, the entire kiosk revolves and sanitizes the interior (a good reason to avoid rushing in after the previous user in an effort to save two francs).

Religion

France is so thoroughly Roman Catholic that they list the saint's day along with next day's weather report. This does not mean that the French are particularly prudish (see above), nor that they attend church. However, they do observe traditions and celebrate the Catholic holidays. If you want to attend services, Catholic or otherwise, you'll find churches of all types in Paris, some with services in English.

Dogs

Don't call the waiter to complain that there's a dog sharing your table—unless he's gobbling your food. Most French bars and cafés accept canine visitors. Food stores usually have signs kindly requesting that best friends stay outside. These are just as kindly ignored by many French who plop Fido into the shopping cart and continue unperturbed. If you love your buddy that much, you'll also be pleased to learn that most hotels accept dogs (ask when you make reservations) so it'll be easy to tour the country together.

> *The Inspector of Schools wanted to take away one of our teachers…*
> *The parents went to Valence, the county seat, to meet with the officials,*
> *arranging an appointment at 5 p.m. to demonstrate. The French are*
> *nothing if not structured. Further plans were made to include a sit-in,*
> *with two mothers at a time sitting in the school. Classes continued*
> *as usual, but the statement was made.*
> —Margo, Rémuzat

Making a Point: Strikes

Periodically students, farmers, workers, or any other group, formal or informal, will demonstrate or go on strike. Occasionally truckers will line their rigs up and slowly, very slowly, clog an autoroute or stop to block it entirely. Farmers will feed the highways with mounds of cabbages or potatoes. *Métro* and train employees will walk instead of driving.

The majority of people resign themselves to working around the problems caused by strikes. The only time to be concerned is when you have to use a missing train or, worse, you're the one behind the load of produce.

At least you'll get free cabbages.

6
Social Occasions

The real reason to live long-term overseas is to involve yourself with new people, make friends from around the world, and become part of a different culture, rather than watching monuments pass in a blur from the tour bus.

How do you meet your neighbors and make friends in France? Basically you do so the same way you would in the States, except that you don't have a ready-made base of family and other friends to grease the wheels. In any totally new environment, you'll need to be outgoing and take the initiative.

Meeting English Speakers

Your ears will perk up at the sound of English being spoken at the grocery store. If the people look like good candidates for friends, you can always find an excuse to introduce yourself politely.

Be aware that just because someone speaks English they may not necessarily be a bosom buddy. Don't leave your senses behind and get too close to people too quickly. I still remember a time we met a woman in a small convenience store and commented that the local English speakers met in the bar next door on Fridays. Oops. It was the beginning of countless hints for entertainment, requests for rides to the next town, and strange comments, such as how lovely it was to sunbathe *au naturel* at her house beside the train tracks.

American Social Organizations

Formal organizations provide an easy means to make contact with other Americans or English-speaking expatriates. Most of these are situated in Paris, Provence, and other areas where English speakers settle in large numbers.

A few of the specifically American organizations include:

American Citizens Abroad (ACA). A group promoting American interests overseas in countries around the world. Contact ACA, 5 bis rue Liotard, CH-1202 Geneva, Switzerland; telephone/fax: (41-22) 340 0233; e-mail: *acage@aca.ch*; website: *http://www.aca.ch.*

American Club of Paris. This group caters to business, diplomatic, arts, and media honchos. The club arranges for prominent speakers, gala dinners, and golf tournaments. Members are screened and sponsored by other members. Contact American Club of Paris, 34, avenue New York, 75016 Paris; telephone: 01 47 23 64 36; fax: 01 47 23 66 01; e-mail: *113146.1231@compuserve.com.*

American Library in Paris. It's a library but also a source for social ineraction, since the group presents speakers and holds special events. Located at 10, rue du Général Camou, 75007 Paris; telephone: 01 45 51 46 82; fax: 01 45 50 25 83.

Association of American Residents Overseas (AARO). Since 1973, AARO has worked to take action on laws made by the U.S. government that affect Americans who reside overseas, including issues of taxation, absentee voting, Social Security, and more. They hold events, such as speaker evenings, and offer group medical insurance. Membership is 390 FF ($65) for an individual, 500 FF ($83) for couples. Contact AARO, BP 127, 92154 Suresnes Cedex; telephone: 01 42 04 09 38; fax: 01 42 04 09 12; e-mail: *aaroparis@aol.com.*

Lions Club International. Philanthropic group known for its work for the blind. Located at 295 rue Saint-Jacques, 75005 Paris; telephone: 01 46 34 14 10; fax: 01 46 33 92 41.

Musée d'Art Américain. The museum features American art created in France, with a special interest in artists of Monet's time. The group has a broader interest in French and American culture and presents special events, concerts, plays, and conferences in English. Located at 99 rue Claude Monet, 27620 Giverny; telephone: 02 32 51 94 65; fax: 02 32 51 94 67.

Rotary Club of Paris. Humanitarian association. Located at 40 boulevard Emile Augier, 75116 Paris; telephone: 01 45 04 14 44. Rotary International: 01 45 0326 20.

WICE. This nonprofit association for the English-speaking community in Paris offers a wide range of continuing education classes and cultural programs. Contact WICE, 20 boulevard du Montparnasse, 75015 Paris; *Métro:* Duroc-Falguière. Telephone 01 45 66 75 50; fax: 01 40 65 96 53; e-mail: *wice@wice-paris.org*; website: *http://www.wice-paris.org.*
YMCA/YWCA. Social and sports group located at 33, rue de Naples, 75008 Paris; telephone: 01 47 20 44 02.

> *The longer I live here, the more I'm attached to my American friends,*
> *with whom I have the most natural rapport. I have more and more*
> *French friends with whom a relationship has grown deeper,*
> *especially now that I can communicate in French.*
>
> —Adrian, Paris

MAKING FRENCH FRIENDS

Becoming involved with the community will introduce you to your neighbors, all of whom are potential friends. Choose activities that you would enjoy, like a local art group or sports club, and friendships will develop naturally, especially as your French improves.

Conversation groups in Paris and other large cities have a dual purpose, since they provide an opportunity for discussion and friendship between French and English speakers.

Accueil des Villes Française

One of the best-kept secrets among English-speaking newcomers to France is the welcome group called *Accueil des Villes Française.* The national organization has 600 groups in towns throughout France, which are called by the town name—for example, *Blois Accueil.* The group's purpose is to provide a center for newcomers to socialize. This group includes both relocating natives and welcomes foreigners as well. Since the goal is to be friendly to newcomers, the people who work in this organization are especially warm and welcoming.

Activities differ, depending on the facilities and personnel available within each volunteer group, but often include language, art, cooking classes, bridge, choral groups, sports, group travel, and social events. Though the *Accueil* system is little known and underutilized by Americans living in France, it's a terrific way to get involved and practice your French—without spending a fortune.

The annual membership fee is just 90 FF ($15). The groups vary in class fees. Some don't charge at all for individual classes; others charge anything from 70 cents to $27 for specific courses.

To find an *Accueil* group near you, ask at the nearest town hall (*mairie*), since they work closely with *Accueil* groups. Or check the yellow pages under *Associations, organismes culturels et socio-éducatifs*.

ENTERTAINING EVENTS

Some books on French culture state that the French entertain in restaurants and rarely at home, implying that the American will never see the inside of a French *maison*. If this is true, you can't prove it by me because I've been entertained in countless French homes, even as a newcomer. Perhaps this is because we live in the country, and the homes are larger.

It's true that in Paris, where kitchens are approximately two meters square, you'll likely be entertained in restaurants. It has nothing to do with friendliness, just facilities.

If you are invited to an event at a person's home, you can't go wrong with taking a good bottle of wine or flowers. Here are a few of the common social events you may attend or even host yourself.

Apéritif Hour
Since French meals are grand and lengthy, hosting one is a major feat. This is one reason that *apéritifs* are so popular. An *apéritif* is a drink before dinner, but it's also the name used for the cocktail party. An *apéritif* can be as simple as a few expats getting together in jeans around several bottles of the local red, or as elaborate as the French version, in which carefully prepared hors d'oeuvres are served formally by the hostess.

Sunday Dinner
The most elaborate meal by far in France is Sunday lunch, which is served at noon or one. Sunday offers more time to sit, relax, and spread out the meal. Don't plan on doing anything afterwards. The meal will last until five or longer. For the rest of the day, you won't be hungry or ready to do anything more strenuous than take a nap.

Randonnée
These are walks or bike rides that are done *en masse*, with a set itinerary that's provided for all participants. In recent years, these events have become very popular in certain areas of the French countryside. You'll see posters, articles in the local paper, or notices at your local *mairie*. Those interested in attending simply show up at the appointed time and place and pay a nominal fee. Each person receives a map and sets off in small groups to follow the path.

The *randonnée* is not a race, just an enjoyable outing, a chance to get exercise and be sociable. As is often the case in France, food and more socializing is involved at some point—either as a lunch break, if it's a long *randonnée*, or at the end of a short one.

Art Openings

France is a country of artists, professional, amateur, and wannabee. Throughout Paris and the smallest towns, art shows are constantly opening and closing. The openings are called *vernissages*, at which artists entertain patrons and friends with champagne or wine and a few treats. If you're fortunate enough to be invited to one, enjoy the art enthusiastically and use the opportunity to mingle and meet new people.

The members of our local art association have already figured out which art gallery has the best bubbly and hors d'oeuvres. That's the one we never miss.

LE BON MOT: SOCIALIZING

Accueil.	Welcome
Apéritif	Cocktail/cocktail party
Cotisation	Membership fee
Déjeuner	Lunch
Dîner.	Dinner
Heure	Time (of an event)
Membre.	Member
Randonnée	Organized walk/bike ride
Soirée	Party
Vernissage	Art opening

GUESTS IN YOUR *CHAMBRE D'AMIS*

When you live in France, you'll discover that your friends and family love having you here. They have someone to run interference for them—someone who understands French and can provide the guided tour and free room and board. Who could possibly pass this deal up? Most don't.

The ability to handle guests depends on your sociability and accommodations. You'll discover that, while you love having visitors, there comes a point when the fourth set of guests (all having arrived in rapid succession) leaves your washing machine huffing and puffing in exhaustion. And you along with it.

We all love company, but having ground rules is essential. If not, you'll soon find yourself being a tour guide for other people's vacations, while having no energy or money left for the activities you came to France to enjoy. And make no mistake, having guests is more than providing the bed. Many of your guests will arrive with no idea what they want to do. Or worse, if you live in the countryside, with no rental car they're stranded without you—and they want to see it all, all the time.

Here are a few tips from Americans with guest rooms in France.

Make Recommendations...but Don't Take Responsibility

If asked, you will certainly be pleased to suggest local sites. Just be careful not to become so embroiled in the planning that your guests assume you'll be the tour guide for their entire two-week vacation.

It helps if you have some literature for guests to read, with maps to help them find their way around. Some people collect brochures in a folder or album so guests can thumb quickly through information about local sites and plan their day trips.

> *People call and say they'll be here in France and thought they'd "stop by."*
> *But I never take "reservations," except from our kids. Promising to be here*
> *months in advance is too difficult, because it commits us to being here,*
> *even if we get an opportunity to take off on an impulse ourselves.*
> —Christine, Loire Valley

Make Sure Visitors Plan Transportation

If you live in Paris, transportation is no problem, since guests can walk or ride the *Métro*. But if you live in the countryside, guests may be stranded without a car, making you the designated driver. And remember, these people just paid for round-trip tickets to France, and they want to pack everything they can into these two weeks. Meanwhile you just want to go back to your garden or put your feet up.

Guests Contribute

This is the stickiest wicket around. Good guests realize that they're getting free accommodations, while you're providing a week's worth of extra meals. This is a lot of work, not to mention money. They'll offer to buy some of the groceries or take you to dinner.

It goes without saying that they should clean up after themselves, assist with preparing meals, and offer to help you clean up. If they seem remiss in volunteering, you can always ask nicely. Sometimes you get stuck with bad guests. The only recourse you have is to be "out of town" the next time they call to visit. And they will, believe me, they will.

> *In the bugbear class...were guests who woke us at 1 a.m. in the morning*
> *because they couldn't manage the key. (The door was unlocked.)*
> —Margot, Drôme Provençale

7
Wining and Dining

ALL HUMAN HISTORY ATTESTS
THAT HAPPINESS FOR MAN—THE HUNGRY SINNER!—
SINCE EVE ATE APPLES, MUCH DEPENDS ON DINNER.
—George Noel Gordon, Lord Byron

If fast food is your idea of a good meal, don't set even one *pied* in France. The truly happy meal in this country takes no less than five courses and a minimum of two hours—triple that if the diners are an especially congenial group.

Dining is an art form in France, one in which the ideal elements include perfectly cooked, seasoned, and sauced cuisine, a well-matched wine, a gracious setting and ambiance, and conversation of fellow diners who are equally interested in the experience.

Naturally, most of the aforementioned conversation centers around previous meals, the proper preparation, and enjoyment of the meal at hand. All of this, as mentioned, takes time. But with such wonderful food, there's not much incentive to leave the table.

At first, you may be impatient with the length of meals when dining out, but you'll soon adapt. On our last trip back to the States, we ate dinner out with friends several times and actually felt rushed with a meal that lasted only an hour and a half.

DINING OUT

One of the most pleasant aspects of dining where you live in France is collecting special dining spots. These are the restaurants where you know the *proprietaire* and thus get a presidential welcome and the table by the window (the one that doesn't wobble).

The other treat about living in France is that you learn insider tips on which local restaurants have special deals. One of the finest restaurants in our neck of the *fôret* is just seven miles from us. The restaurant is worth every *centime*, but insiders know to plan their visits for Monday through Thursday nights. Those are the nights that a special 98-franc menu is offered. That's about $16 for four melt-in-your-mouth courses.

One way to cut costs is to dine out, as many French people do, with the main meal at lunch, since the same meal is much less expensive at midday. Or choose *le menu*, which is the name for a combination of courses that, if purchased together, rates a special price. (Note that what we call the menu in the States, the list of the restaurant's offerings, is called *la carte* in France.)

A pauper's budget has prevented me from testing Michelin Guide listings, but not from ferreting out little "momma-poppa" restaurants in neighborhoods to discover great meals at a great price.
—Adrian, Paris

All restaurants post their *menus* outside, so you can note the specials of the day and plan your meal in advance. Usually you'll have a choice. *Le menu* can include an *entrée* (starter), *plat* (main dish), *fromage* (cheese course) and/or *dessert* (dessert). Sometimes there are different combinations, such as starter and main dish or main dish and dessert, for the set price. Beverages are usually priced separately, but occasionally a *menu* will include wine or coffee. The *entrée* in France is the "entrance" to the meal—the first course. Don't confuse it with the U.S. version, which means the main course. In France, the main course is called *le plat*.

Dark French coffee comes in demitasse cups after dinner in France. That's *after* dinner. The French take meals in stages, and coffee is served at the end as its own course. Americans order coffee and expect it to arrive with dessert. In France, even if you make a big point about having coffee with dessert, this will probably confuse your waiter and he still can't bring himself to serve it at the "wrong" time. If you're lucky, it'll come with a chocolate on the saucer.

Choosing Your Table

French sidewalk cafés are designed to showcase the human parade outside. Tables just big enough to balance an espresso cup or a wine glass manage to attract hordes of bistro-style chairs. Note that they're all lined up in one direction—facing the street. The sidewalk is the moving picture of life, better than any Hollywood extravaganza, and the French wouldn't miss a minute of it. Sit down, order, and you're free to ogle the passersby. Food and drink cost more when you sit at a table outside, as opposed to standing at the counter. But no one will hassle you for lingering as long as you like. Terrace seats are like a first-class seat in a plane. You get a special space, and you pay a little more.

LE BON MOT: DINING OUT

Addition	The bill
Carte	Menu
Couverts	Place setting
Dessert	Dessert
Entrée	Starter
Menu	Fixed-priced meal
Plat	Main course
Serveur/serveuse	Waiter/waitress

Ordering

If you have questions about the way a dish is prepared, you can ask your waiter. When you select *le menu*, you'll make your selections from the courses offered and normally there are no substitutions. However, if you order the top-priced menu and prefer the lower-priced dessert, they'll certainly accommodate you. If you want to pick and choose, then order *à la carte* as separate dishes.

For meats, specify the degree of doneness. This is essential if you do not like rare meats, since rare is the normal cooking style in France. You can choose to have meats cooked *à point* (medium) or *bien cuit* (medium well).

Butter is rarely served with the bread. If you must have it, ask. Salt and pepper may or may not be on the table. Some French people claim it's an insult to the chef to use it!

Types of Restaurants

You'll find many wonderful places to eat in France but few are called "restaurant." Below is a brief list of some of the distinctions.

Auberge	An inn, usually casual, although some fine dining places also use the term. *Ferme auberge* is a farm restaurant with home cooking.
Bar	The place for a casual drink, coffee, or soft drinks.
Bistro	Small and family-run; often the husband is the chef, and the wife acts as hostess and waitress.

Brasserie	Tends to be larger than a café and often serves food all day.
Café	A restaurant with casual dining and a small selection of meals.
Restaurant	A dining establishment serving full meals.
Salon de Thé	Combines a pastry shop with a few luncheon-style dishes such as *quiche.* Good for a quick and easy meal.
Zinc	Another name for a bar.

I Shudder to Say It...Fast Foods

McDonald's and Burger King and Domino's exist in France, along with various French fast-food equivalents, such as Quick. However, in the traditional French restaurant, the long *déjeuner* (lunch) or *dîner* (dinner) is *normale.* So "grabbing a bite" to eat doesn't translate at all to a French waiter.

If you're rushing to make a train or see the next *château*, don't sit down in a restaurant. You'll simply make yourself and the waiter miserable, since a normal restaurant isn't equipped for rushed diners. Instead, select a place that serves good food quickly.

Salons de thé (tea rooms) serve *quiche* and other light dishes that are already prepared, so they're usually fast. Some *bistros* serve meals more quickly, though not always. If you're seriously pressed for time, *boulangeries* (bakeries) often fill fresh French bread with cheese or ham—which they call *le sandwich.* Or run in a *charcuterie* for *paté*, a *fromagerie* for cheese, a *boulangerie* for bread, and make your own sandwich. Fast food never tasted so good.

Time Warp

Do Americans eat too fast? Or do the French eat too slowly? Whichever, many times I've tapped my fingers, toes, and my husband's shoulder to ask him to catch the waiter's eye for the check. This is a typical American response. It's also a typical American response to assume that you're being ignored on purpose. (Hence that misguided "arrogant" French reputation again.)

Sure, it *could* be lackadaisical service or a personal insult, but that's not likely. Usually, it's the exact opposite: *The waiter is being polite.*

Since dining is practically a religious experience in France, waiters deliberately take their time to avoid rushing you. Many a time a meal has taken three hours—and those are the normal ones. Our record is five and a half hours.

When you're ready for the bill, it may be necessary to ask, "*L'addition, s'il vous plaît.*" Or just make a scribbling motion on your palm. That's universal.

A Tip to Avoid Double Tipping

In France, the majority of restaurants include tips in the price of the meal. This is called *service compris*, literally service included. To check if the restaurant has done this, look for the words *service compris* or the initials *SC* or *STC* (that's tax included too) at the bottom of the menu. If you don't see it, you can ask your waiter, "*Service est compris?*" (*Serre-vees eh cohm-pree?*) Hopefully, he or she will be honest about it.

However, it's safe to say that ninety-nine percent of the time service is included in France. Though not required, you can leave small change to round up the bill. In the (very) unusual case that service is not included, tip ten to fifteen percent of the total.

Not all restaurants take credit cards—especially some small, family-run establishments. If relying on this method of payment, check for credit card symbols before you eat crow.

THE WINE LIST

You don't have to be a wine connoisseur to choose a good wine in France. Nor do you have to be rich. Just select the local French wine, which is usually served in a small pitcher and called a *pichet*. Half that serving is a *demi-pichet*. A quarter is a *quart-pichet*. Such table wines will have been selected from a local vintner who's a neighbor or even a relative of the *propriétaire*. They're usually quite good.

What's amazing to those of us who used to consider wine a splurge with a special dinner is that wine in France is the norm. It not only tastes better, it costs far less than a soft drink, juice, or beer.

For this reason, it's tempting to indulge yourself, but remember to enjoy wine in moderation. Despite their love of wine, the French abhor drunkenness. They drink their wine slowly, often alternating with water. As with anywhere, don't drive after drinking. Not only do you need all your wits about you on French roads, but *les gendarmes* test blood alcohol and acceptable levels are even lower than in the States.

APÉRITIFS AND SPECIAL DRINKS

An *apéritif* is not one drink, but the name for the general category of drinks served before dinner. *Apéritif* is also used as the name for a cocktail party. Occasionally hard liquor, such as a whiskey, will be offered, but these days the drink of choice appears to be a sparkling wine or a *kir*. The hostess will pass platters of finger foods, such as a meat or fish *paté* spread on thin slices of French bread or small filled appetizers called *amuse-gueules* or *amuse-bouches* (literally means to amuse the throat or the mouth).

Champagne and Sparkling Wine
True champagne can only be called that if it's from the region of Champagne. However, if you like bubbly, you can also choose *méthode traditionelle* or *pétillante*. The former is created with the same loving hand-turning of the bottles as champagne, but just not in the Champagne region. The latter is a sparkling wine that's been produced by more modern machine methods, not the traditional ones.

Kir
One of the favorite *apéritifs* of France is *kir*. It's a combination of about a quarter wine glass of *cassis*, a tasty black currant liqueur, topped with white wine. A *kir royale* is champagne or sparkling wine with cassis. A version of a *kir* can also be made with peach or pear liqueur.

Here we'll admit a small *faux pas* of our own. Once, in line at one of our favorite Paris bistros, we wanted a drink. My husband ordered wine and was handed a *kir*. He started to complain that it wasn't what he had ordered. His face turned *rouge* when he discovered the generous owner was offering a free *kir* to those in line while they waited. Oops.

Martini
Not to be confused with the American cocktail, Martini is a fortified wine popular in France as an *apéritif* before meals. You can order it *rouge* (red), *rosé* (pink), or *blanc* (white). If you want the kind of martini that comes with an olive or a lemon twist, order a *martini américain.*

Pastis
Pastis is a strong *apéritif* for those who devoured licorice sticks when they were kids, though if you really, really like licorice flavor, beware. This stuff packs a lot more punch.

Calvados
Made from apples, *calvados* brandy is a particular favorite in the Normandy region of France. You can buy other forms of apple drinks in Normandy as well, including *cidre* (cider), which may or may not be alcoholic.

LE BON MOT: AT THE BAR

Bière	Beer (in a bottle)
Café	Coffee
Café allongé	Coffee with extra hot water (to dilute the strength)
Café au lait	Very light coffee (lots of milk)
Café crème	Large coffee with milk
Express	Small cup of strong black coffee
Kir	Cassis and white wine
Kir royale	Cassis and champagne
Martini	A popular brand of fortified wine
Pétillante	Sparkling (water or wine)
Pichet	Pitcher (usually applied to house wine)
Pression	Beer on draft
Sans alcool	No alcohol (beer)
Thé	Tea
Vin blanc	White wine
Vin rouge	Red wine

LIFESTYLES: RETIRED IN WINE COUNTRY

In central France, a few hours from Paris, lies a lengthy stretch of quiet river valleys, undulating with vineyards, forests and peaceful small towns. The area holds little in the way of major industry, but that's ideal for the Americans who have retired there, those who'd just as soon keep the area *tranquille.*

"It's pretty but what do you do all day?" asked a visitor to John Luther's rented farmhouse. There isn't a mall or movie theater for miles.

The American considers his typical day: He's up at eight, but there's no use in rushing anything, so he has his Special K along with the news on France 2 as language practice. If it's a market day in town, he grabs a large *panier* and strolls the stalls, working on the serious business of planning meals in France. Normally, he spends the morning talking with merchants and friends in town while filling his basket with the season's fresh produce—radishes, asparagus, green beans, and goat cheese.

On some days, he may visit only his favorite stalls and make the selections quickly, because the sun's bright, and he's planned a long bike ride. An interlacing complex of small roads threads through the vineyards, forests, and small hamlets. There's little traffic other than the wine tractor chugging its way to the cooperative. "I can always tell when I'm getting close to one of the wine caves," he says. "One vintner in particular stores his wine in massive stainless steel tanks near the street, and it smells downright intoxicating."

One favorite ride takes him an hour and a half; he takes a lunch break at a small café in the shadow of the château at Chaumont. Refreshed by a simple sandwich of ham or the local *rillettes* (a soft paste of cooked pork) on fresh baguettes, he begins to bike along the Loire River. As an amateur painter, he can't resist stopping at a park bench to sketch the scene.

At home, it's time to make soup with that snow-white cauliflower he found at market that morning. It's ready for tomorrow's lunch, but tonight he's invited for dinner at the home of some other Americans who live in the next town. At home after midnight, he settles down to relax with the *International Herald Tribune* that he didn't have time to read earlier. He dozes off at one in the morning with a smile on his face.

"The days fly by so fast," he says. "I don't understand how anyone can think my life is boring when there's so much here to just plain enjoy!"

8
The Market Basket

HOW CAN YOU BE EXPECTED TO GOVERN A COUNTRY
THAT HAS 246 KINDS OF CHEESE?
—Charles de Gaulle

Market stalls in France rank right up there with the Eiffel Tower for thrills. Actually, they're better, because you can visit the Tower just so often, but you need to eat three times a day.

Buying fresh ingredients, then creating your own meals, is the true joy of cooking. Everything tastes better—yes, even spinach. The first time I tasted spinach fresh from a French farm, I wasn't expecting much except a healthy vegetable rich in iron to go with our chicken dinner. I expected to have to doctor the spinach with butter to make it palatable. But these particular dark green leaves were rich in taste, aromatic, and absolutely delicious. The butter stayed in the fridge.

Fresh vegetables that were growing in the French countryside a few hours before you purchased them at a market stall will be more flavorful than you can ever imagine. You'll want to shop in the local markets whenever possible.

The nice thing about chicken here is that it's not shrouded in plastic and hasn't spent half its dead life in trucks.
—Judith, Paris

STREET SHOPPING

Street markets are packed with straw baskets and pull-carts owned by the shoppers who stroll up and down the temporary stands. Each town of any size holds a market one morning or afternoon each week for the local farmers who turn the town square or several streets into fresh-air shopping.

You'll see quail and sausages and chickens with the heads still on—the better to guarantee the type of chicken you're buying. (They'll remove the head and cut up the chicken for you if you ask.)

Pick and choose from whatever's available that season. Endive is available in winter (great braised as a side dish or in an endive/walnut/Roquefort salad). White asparagus is available in spring. Sweet cherries are available in early summer. Whatever the selection, take advantage of your region's specialties during the in-season, when these items are less expensive and taste better.

Do some comparison shopping for freshness and price. Watch where the locals line up, and you'll find the best quality and value.

My favorite activity with visitors is market.
I love to see their faces if they've never seen one before. It's fascinating!
—Karen, Loire Valley

Packaging and the Lack Thereof

In the *boulangerie* don't be surprised when the clerk thrusts a naked loaf of bread at you. Bags are rare, though a small piece of paper may encircle the middle. Do as the French do; just tuck a *baguette* under your arm or wrap it loosely in a piece of your morning paper.

In countless village markets you'll see mussels, salmon, chicken, veal, beef, cheeses, olives, and pastries sitting on tables in all their bare glory. This astounds some Americans. An acquaintance went so far as to warn us: "Be careful. I hear they don't offer packaged or frozen food."

Right. It's called *fresh*.

CHOCOHOLICS, TAKE NOTE

Chocolate in France is *le vrai* thing; it contains a higher percentage of cocoa than what Americans consider chocolate. While the common bar in the United States may contain only 2% cocoa, French chocolates brag of their 70% or even 76% cocoa. These chocolates melt wonderfully for baking and in the mouth. Plus, according to popular French wisdom, the greater the cocoa percentage, the better chocolate is for your health. Chocoholics like me believe it.

Living to Eat?

Every region in France has its specialities. Why not consider your own tastes when choosing a location to live? Here are a few areas (regions or cities) and the delicacies for which they're known.

Apples & cider . . . . Normandy

Brandy . . . . Cognac

Butter and cream . . . . Normandy

Chocolate . . . . Lyons, the old town

Foie gras . . . . Dordogne and the southwest

Ham . . . . Bayonne

Melon . . . . Cavaillon (Provence)

Mushrooms . . . . Loire Valley

Olives . . . . Provence

Truffles . . . . Provence

Wild game . . . . Sologne/Loire Valley

Wine . . . . Bordeaux
                        Burgundy
                        Provence
                        OK, anywhere at all

Specialty Food Shops

You can't find everything in the local market. Small shops will be family-run and are specialized, as are the market stands. You'll go from one to the other to select your meat, fish, vegetables, and bread.

The small shops are most likely owned by couples or families and therefore tend to close at lunch time. Hours are approximately nine to noon or twelve-thirty, opening again from two, two-thirty, or even three until seven or so. They will usually be closed a day during the week, Sundays, and holidays, though the store may be open Sunday mornings and close at noon. These stores close for the owners' vacation. You'll just have to double-check the hours of your favorite shops until it becomes second nature.

Below is a guide to the different kinds of shops and what you'll find in each.

Boucherie

The butcher's shop. You'll find fresh cuts of meat (including many you've never heard of). All meats are the cook-it-yourself kind, which differentiates this type of establishment from a *charcuterie*.

Boulangerie
Bread, in all its shapes, is found here. It's fresh and fairly priced. The price of traditional breads is regulated by law—probably because the last person who got huffy about bread was Marie Antoinette. When French peasants complained they couldn't afford it, she stated, "Let them eat cake"; needless to say, she lost her head.

Charcuterie
This is the place to find cooked delicacies such as spiced meats, *paté*, quiches, omelets, pizza—all of which are ideal for a picnic.

Confiserie
The word for calorie in French is recognizable as *calorie*. You can buy *kilos* of them in these sweet shops. Try the chocolates—both dark and white. Certain regions have their own specialties, such as the almond-paste *calissons* in Provence.

Epicerie (or Alimentation)
Here, you can buy water, soft drinks, fruit juice, and a range of products. It is a small general store.

Fromagerie
France supposedly has more than 365 varieties of cheeses, one for each day of the year. They're mild or powerful, creamy or dry, and so rich and mouthwatering, it will make your cholesterol rise just contemplating them.

Pâtisserie
Don't go here first, or you'll blow your whole lunch budget on the array of perfectly arranged, glazed tarts and other pastries—and waste your time in France shopping for larger clothes.

Poissonnerie
No, they're not trying to poison ugly Americans. This is a fish shop.

It's the Real Thing: AOC
You'll see the initials AOC, which stands for *Appellation d'origine contrôlée*, on wine bottles and food items such as cheese, poultry, and some vegetables. These items have strict controls on region, means of production, and quality.

It's so much more fun—and good for one's French—to shop in the small stores. My butcher would discuss the differences in chickens, even when my French wasn't that great, as long as I bought one!

—Judith, Paris

Super and Hypermarkets

Large supermarkets or hypermarkets that have a wide selection of food items plus clothing and other general merchandise, will offer promotions with good prices, though the produce won't usually be as fresh. Like U.S. supermarkets, the food is trucked in. However, some supermarkets have excellent fish or bakeries. You will need to experiment to see what the options are near you.

Most supermarkets require you to weigh your own fruits and vegetables at the produce department before carting them to the check-out. We kept forgetting to do this, until having to run back to produce—leaving people in line behind us—eventually sealed the habit into our brains.

In many places in France you're expected to bring your own reusable bags, though this is changing; now most stores provide plastic bags. You will need to bag the groceries yourself, as there are no baggers in France. Load the conveyor belt, then, as your groceries are scanned, move to the end and begin quickly bagging. Once everything's done, the clerk will tell you the price, and you'll pay.

A Coin for a Cart

Isn't it shocking that those lines of shopping carts outside the French supermarkets cost ten francs to use? Not really, since you get your money back. Just put a ten-franc coin into the slot, and the cart springs free for shopping. When you return the cart and lock it back into place, the coin pops out. It's a simple system that virtually eliminates car-dinging carts in the parking lot.

Finding American-Style Foods

Planning Thanksgiving dinner and can't find real, honest-to-goodness cranberries? Looking for Crisco to make the pie crust *à l'américain*? Your chances increase if you live in Paris, where stores cater to the large English-American population.

Thanksgiving is a store that's appropriately named for the day when you're most likely to want cranberries and other similar foods. It offers the largest selection of imported U.S. groceries in Paris. It's open Tuesday through Sunday, 11 a.m. to 7 p.m. You'll find Thanksgiving year round at

14, rue Charles V, 75004, Paris; for information or telephone orders, call 01 42 77 68 29.

Louisiana-Cajun food is served in Thanksgiving's restaurant, which is next door, but you enter around the corner at 20, rue St. Paul, 75004; call for times or reservations: 01 42 77 68 28.

The Real McCoy. Sells American brand-name food products, including those basic cooking products for American-style cakes and pies, at 194, rue de Grenelle, 75007 Paris. *Métro:* École Militaire; telephone: 01 45 56 98 82.

To find American-style foods outside Paris, visit one of the large hypermarkets. They usually have a section with imported foods.

WINES BY THE BARREL

Living in France offers a major advantage over a short visit: You're not limited to taking home a few bottles of wine. You can buy liters and liters of the stuff *en vrac* (in bulk), bottle it yourself, and stock your own wine cave for a fraction of the cost.

Not that wine is that costly in France to begin with, but $1.25 a bottle is a real steal. We've bought Chinons this way that we know would have been $10 or more in the States. Even the world-famous Gigondas (okay, so this worked out to $3 a bottle) sits in our wine cave with homemade labels.

In wine country, stop by the vineyards and wine *coopératives* that advertise their *caves*, which is a wine cellar, as having *dégustation*, which means "tasting." *Gratuit(e)* means free. However, it's polite to taste only if you're serious about buying something. *Dégustation* is not meant to be a free cocktail hour.

A plastic jug called a *cubitainer* (nicknamed a *cubie*) holds five or ten liters of wine. These jugs are filled with a hose from the huge wine tanks. You'll be buying the previous year's wine, which, depending on the type of wine, will be drinkable now or may be kept for years of aging once it's bottled.

When you purchase wine this way, the wine must be approved for transit. The vintner will either provide his own sealed *cubitainer*, fill and seal yours, or fill your *cubitainer* and supply a VA2 form, which indicates the wine purchase, quantity, date and your vehicle's license number, and the amount of time the wine will be in transit to your home. (You can exaggerate the time since they expect you to dawdle along the way.)

Wine-bottling supplies, such as a simple corking machine, bottles, corks, and labels, are available in large hardware stores, hypermarkets, and wine specialty shops.

Now You're Cooking

You have the rosy tomatoes, the ripe avocado, the perfect filet of fish. Now it's time to prepare that fabulous meal. This is up to you and your taste buds, but a few tips are in order.

> Cooking even the relatively simple meal takes stamina.
> It's not the cooking so much as finding the right pan and comparing
> value for price (because kitchen equipment can be astronomical).
> [It's a challenge] figuring out substitutions for the ingredients our
> American recipes call for, but that don't exist here.
> —Betsy, the Dordogne

Equipment

First of all, your cookbooks will most likely be American style-with standard (not metric) weights and measures. These are not easy to convert. Even if you don't move your entire household, bring U.S. measuring cups and spoons, plus any special pans. It took me four trips to different stores to find a bundt pan that would be close to the one I needed for an American-style recipe. Regular pie pans don't exist in France either. Their pies are *tartes*, and the pans are different. (Finding Crisco for the pie crust is virtually impossible in my corner of France anyway, unless I have a friend bring it from Paris.)

Converting Recipes

France uses the metric system of weights and measures, which takes some adjusting for U.S. recipes. Here are some of the helpful conversions.

	U.S.	*Metric*
Weights:		
	1 oz.	28.35 grams (g)
	1 pound (16 oz)	454 grams (g)
	2.2 pounds	1 kilo (kg)
Liquids:		
	1 cup	250 milliliters (ml)
	4 cups/1 quart	1 liter (l)
	1 pint	47 liters (*litres*)
	1 gallon	3.78 liters (*litres*)

> You have to experiment with American recipes here,
> because even basics like flour, brown sugar, and butter are different.
> It's fun in one way but frustrating when cookies turn out flat!
> —Judith, Paris

Oven Temperatures

Baking temperatures in France are given in Celsius or as a single-digit thermostat setting. To convert Fahrenheit to Celsius, subtract 32, multiply by 5, and divide by 9—or just copy this chart of approximate equivalencies and keep it near your oven. Note that not every oven is accurate. You may have to experiment with yours.

Fahrenheit	Celsius	Oven #
275	135	1
300	150	2
325	160	3
350	180	4
375	190	5
400	200	6
425	220	7
450	230	8
475	245	9
500	260	10

LE BON MOT: COOKING TERMS

Items:

Boite . . . . Can
Casserole . . . . Saucepan
Cocotte . . . . Casserole dish
Poêle . . . . Frying pan

Measurements:

Cuillière/cuillière a café . . . . . Teaspoon
Cuillière a soupe . . . . Tablespoon
Litre . . . . Liter

Actions:

Ajouter . . . . Add (an ingredient)
Arroser . . . . Baste
Baiser . . . . Braise
Bouillir . . . . Boil
Cuire au four . . . . To bake in the oven
Fouetter . . . . Beat
Frire . . . . To fry
Mélanger . . . . To blend
Mijoter . . . . To simmer

9
Home Sweet *Maison*

THE BEST THING WE CAN DO IS TO MAKE WHEREVER WE'RE LOST IN
LOOK AS MUCH LIKE HOME AS WE CAN.
—Christopher Fry, *The Lady's Not for Burning* (1949)

Readying your home in France is a matter of narrowing down the choices. Let's assume you've decided on a region, then a particular city, village, or countryside in that region. Now it's time to settle on the specific home or apartment where you'll lay your head every night.

Since we're assuming here that you are staying in France longer than two weeks, you'll want to find a relatively long-term rental. These are available furnished or unfurnished, though furnished homes and apartments are naturally more expensive; this is especially true in Paris, where they're catering to tourists. What a person's willing to pay for a two-week holiday is distinctly different than what the same person would pay on a year-round basis.

That said, you may still want to search for something furnished, since that saves you from moving furniture until you're sure you want to stay in France long enough to make the move worth your while. Another possibility, however, is to rent an unfurnished apartment or house, and furnish it very simply. You can use the furnishings in another property or sell them later.

Whatever you do, rent first. Don't purchase an apartment or house based on the puppy love that occurs when you first visit France. Purchase costs in the form of *notaire* fees and taxes are steep, so it's well worth your while to be patient. Rent in an area for at least a year, so that you can sample the climate in all seasons, as well as ensure that the local activities are to your liking and that the area is neither too sleepy, nor too crowded in certain seasons.

Size Shock

Americans are accustomed to open spaces but be prepared for coziness in France, especially in Paris, where apartment space is at a premium. One young American wife, who moved to France suddenly due to her husband's corporate transfer, admitted that she cried when she saw the two-bedroom apartment the real estate agent had found for them. Now that she has had a chance to adjust her expectations, she admits it "is plenty of space for just the two of us."

Save yourself some pain by adjusting any Texas-size expectations before beginning the apartment search.

Finding a Rental

One of the best sources for English speakers looking for rental accommodations in Paris is through *France-USA Contacts (FUSAC)*, 3 rue la Rochelle, 75040 Paris; telephone: 01 45 38 56 57; or P.O. Box 115, Cooper Station, NY 10276, USA. This monthly publication is distributed throughout Paris. Its classified section includes furnished and unfurnished apartments, houses for rent and purchase, plus accoutrements, such as appliances sold when other expats are moving back and forth. You can order *FUSAC* and have it mailed to you weekly in the States; the postage fee is $30 for six months, and $55 for a year.

The *Paris Free Voice* is an arts, entertainment, and community newspaper published by the American University in Paris. It often includes ads for housing and holiday rentals. Pick it up free at the American Church, 65 Quai d'Orsay, 75007; telephone: 01 40 62 05 00.

You can check the *International Herald Tribune*, 181 avenue Charles-de-Gaulle, Neuilly-sur-Seine, 92200. However, the properties in this publication are higher-end places in status and cost, usually designed for tourists and businesspeople with expense accounts..

The Women's Institute for Continuing Education (WICE) posts a bulletin board with apartments for rent or sublet, as well as household items for sale. The American Cathedral also has a bulletin board with rentals, house sharing, and sale items.

For a wider range of options in areas throughout France, check classifieds in regional and city papers. These are in French, of course, but since they're short and relatively simple, you should be able to manage.

One of the largest publications dedicated to housing rentals and sales is *De Particulier á Particulier*, which is published weekly. It's available on newsstands and costs 15 FF (about $2.50) a copy. The address is 40 rue du Docteur Roux, 75015 Paris; telephone: 01 40 56 35 35.

Le Journal des Particuliers provides rental and sale listings for 12 francs, or about $2. *Le Figaro* newspaper also has listings, though mostly for Paris.

If you are searching for an apartment in Paris, get the paper while the ink's still wet. The competition for the best Parisian apartments is fierce.

In the French countryside, you'll find much more space for less money. You can rent furnished country homes (*gîtes*) for short-term stays, while you search for something more permanent. Travel agents have books that list *gîtes* by region. They're not designed for long-term leases, but you can rent one for a month or two, depending on the location and management.

We looked at eighteen apartments in four hours, then saw workers going in and out of one, so we investigated. It was being renovated and we took it immediately.
—Amanda, Paris

Reading Want Ads

Apartments in France are often described as F1, F2, F3, or F4, which seems like a complete mystery. However, the numbers correspond to the number of rooms in the apartment, not counting the bathrooms, WC (water closet/toilet), or kitchen. For example, a one-bedroom apartment with living room would be two rooms, designated F2.

Homes are described by the number of bedrooms, living rooms, and other descriptions of the surrounding property, as well as other buildings, such as a garage or barn. The square meters of the house and property are usually provided as well.

A friend here helped us find our house by introducing us to the local facteur de lettres—the postman—and he knew his route inside out. We found the "perfect" place but the owner wanted a three-year lease. After much negotiation, he finally allowed us to lease the two-story stone cottage for a year.
—Betsy, the Dordogne

Rental Agencies

Some rental agencies can help English speakers find a temporary place to live while they look for something more permanent. Two of these include Families Abroad, 194 Riverside Drive, Apt. 6D, New York, NY 10025, (212) 787-2434, which specializes in short-term rentals (three months to a year) and deals primarily with the owners of apartments or houses; Relocation Services, 57 rue Pierre Charron, 75008, telephone: 01 42 89 09 15; fax 01 42 25 35 92) works directly with companies that are transferring families for longer stays. They will provide information and ancillary services, such as helping you buy rental insurance or find a place to store your car. Services range from about 10,000 to 15,000 French francs ($1,660 to $2,500).

You can also go through a French real estate agent, who will charge a finder's fee. Some apartments are totally empty except for the walls, but if they've been improved, you may be requested to pay extra compensation to the previous tenant for the improvements.

LE BON MOT: HOUSING TERMS

Appartement.	Apartment
Bail.	Lease
Charges.	Regular payments for building services
Grand standing.	Luxury apartment building
Locataire.	Renter
Propriétaire.	Owner
Libre de suite.	Immediate occupancy
Loyer.	Rent
Meublé	Furnished
Non-meublé	Unfurnished
Tout confort	All conveniences

Long-Term Leases

A written lease is essential. Before you sign anything, however, be sure you have a written description in the lease of all fixtures that stay in the rental and their condition, the rental fee, and an estimate of all service charges relating to the rental. For example, in Paris buildings, there will often be a concierge, and you'll be charged monthly for the service.

You'll probably need to prove your monthly income, which should be four times the basic rent, or to produce a guarantee from a bank or French citizen. You'll also need to supply a two-month rental deposit and provide insurance for your belongings.

Standard leases in France are for three years, but you can negotiate. In any case, the long lease is designed to protect the renter—not the owner. Renters are responsible for most improvements to unfurnished apartments and homes, so check to see what your responsibilities and rights are for the specific unit.

A *tax d'habitation* (inhabitant's tax) is due January 1 of each year, payable by whoever lives in the apartment as of that date.

What amazed me was that they don't have a sort of
[multi-list] computer system here [for housing]. It's all word of mouth.
—Patricia, Paris

Home Exchange

Though home exchanges are normally for a short term, they offer an inexpensive way for you to have a sabbatical in France—if you are willing to trade your home for someone's in France. This can cut your costs of renting overseas and sometimes provides access to a car or bike. Look for exchangeable homes via business colleagues, friends of friends, classifieds, or professional home exchange directories, or agents. You'll find many exchange offers on the World Wide Web and in travel magazines and newsletters.

To arrange a home exchange, check financial and personal references, set the parameters in advance for how long the exchange will last, and determine whether car, bikes, or boat are included, and how many people or pets will be using your home.

PURCHASING YOUR PIECE OF THE *ROCHER*

Americans and Brits in France eventually fall in love with the strong, silent types—the French country homes. These homes have thick stone walls, massive fireplaces, and sturdy beams that span the length of the rooms. (Actually, we once determined that houses are sized based on the size beams available, which explains why homes are long and narrow.)

The Home-Shopping Network

Real estate is relatively easy to purchase in France and there are no restrictions that prevent an American from purchasing. However, finding your own walls in France takes more adventure than in the States. In France, multilisting services, which enable real estate agents to share information on homes for sale, do not exist. You'll traipse from real estate agent to notary to individuals running ads. When you don't find anything, you'll start all over again. Most of the time you'll enjoy it, for this is your opportunity to take a peek inside those protective hawthorn hedges and massive metal gates topped with spikes. These people actually want you to visit their museumlike homes.

As with rental properties you can search for properties to buy directly through English-language or French sources. *French Property News* is a British-based paper with lots of real estate agency ads and some private sellers (send e-mail to *info@french-property-news.com* or call 0181 947 1834).

If you can read French, check out *De Particulier á Particulier* or *Le Journal des Particuliers,* which are available on newsstands. Also look for classified ads in the local newspapers of the specific area in which you are interested.

See enough homes to be able to compare the values in the area. One thing you'll notice is that prices are not necessarily predicated on decoration in France. The square meters of habitable space are the most important factor in cost of a property. Don't be swayed by a good paint job when making an offer. Ads will note if a property has been updated or *amenagé* or if extra space is available that can be converted into living space.

When you find your dream home, don't let the "potential" blind you. Be sure to have the property inspected. This is a good idea in the United States, of course, but is even more important in France, because French homes are constructed differently than U.S. ones. You might as well have someone who's familiar with the local methods of construction inspect the home for problems.

If you want to restore an old home, be aware that the cost will in many cases equal the purchase price—often much more. Get several estimates before you commit to a purchase that could put you in hot water figuratively, while leaving you with a cold shower. Renovation will also eat into your time in France. You may enjoy working on the home yourself or arranging for its repair. But it's often difficult to get craftsmen to show up and schedule projects. There are just too few of them, and too many old homes. It's nothing to hear that extensive renovation projects have taken upwards of three to nine years to complete.

Of course, you can also buy new or build in France. You'll gain more modernity, but you'll lose all that charm...and the fun of complaining about poky pipes.

We love the old barn we renovated. It's got the best view of the mountains!
—Sara, the Ardèche

LE BON MOT: NAME THAT ROOM!

Bureau	Office
Chambre	Bedroom
Cuisine	Kitchen
Garage	Garage
Jardin	Garden
Pièce	Room
Salle à manger	Dining room
Salon	Living room
Salle de bain	Bathroom
WC	Toilet

Making an Offer

In France, as in the United States, the price stated is not necessarily what you should pay. Since you'll be dealing in a new environment, one in which you don't yet understand the cost comparisons based on location, size, and state of the home, be sure to study want ads and compare and look at several dozen houses—at the very least—before making an offer.

If purchasing an apartment *en copropriété* (joint ownership) you must contribute to the costs of building maintenance. Get the service charges in writing, including costs of a concierge or shared heating systems. Ask to see records of the service charges if you're buying a used apartment.

Your offer can be ten to fifteen percent less than the offer price. Common sense applies. If the house appears to be drastically overpriced, offer much less. If it's a steal, you can still offer less, but try to avoid insulting the owners. We once offered twenty percent less for a house and created a complicated formula for the down payment. We weren't sure about the house, but thought if we could get it for the price, we'd be happy. As it turned out, the owner wouldn't even consider the offer, which was fortunate since our instincts were right, and we never should have made the offer in the first place. We later found a home that fit our needs much better, and we were grateful that we'd actually ruined the deal by making such a low offer.

You can make an offer with a *promesse d'achat* (promise to buy). The seller will sign a *promesse de vent* (promise of sale). This exchange binds you to the agreement. You, as the buyer, will make a down payment of ten percent *dépôt de garantie*, which the notary puts into escrow until the purchase is finalized. This fee covers the cost of the mortgage application, notary and legal fees, and real estate agent commissions. You will forfeit the *dépôt de garantie* if you do not fulfill the *promesse d'achat* so be sure that this is your dream home before you sign it.

If you need a mortgage to purchase the property, check to see that the *promesse d'achat* contains a *clause suspensive de prêt*, which makes the *promesse* dependent upon your obtaining a mortgage. Otherwise, if you can't get financing, you'll lose your deposit.

Get professional legal advice before purchasing the property. French inheritance and tax laws are complex and vary greatly from those in the United States. Note that if and when you sell your French property, you must pay French gains tax.

> *Our house is an old school of the type built all over France*
> *just before and after 1900. These are one-room schoolhouses with*
> *an apartment for the teacher upstairs....We came here for space and light,*
> *so we've kept it as it was, but now the all-in-one room is living room,*
> *dining room, office, sewing room, and kitchen.*
> —Margot, Drôme Provençale

A Buck-Naked House

When homes are sold in France, they are emptied thoroughly before the new owner gains possession. This is Empty with a capital "E." Even those things that are bolted to the walls, and which you might never dream would leave the premises, are up for grabs.

Unless you've made other arrangements with the owners, the light fixtures, fans, cupboards, and, yes, the toilet-paper holder, will be gone, leaving bare wires and pockmarked walls where the toilet-paper holder used to be. This presents the difficulty of finding the exact medicine chest to fill the empty spot or the towel rack that will fit the identical holes. If you want, you can purchase items from the owners. Just make sure you let them know and make it part of the purchase contract, or settle up separately. For example, our sellers left satellite dishes and draperies as part of the contract. We purchased some of the bathroom accessories. Unfortunately, we weren't specific enough and ended up losing a few towel racks and spent weeks, literally, scanning stores for the exact duplicates. Finally, we gave up and settled for a slightly larger size, so that the towels hanging on them hide the holes.

Mortgages

Real estate agents and notaries help you obtain a mortgage as part of the ten percent fee you pay with your *promesse*. Our agent literally walked us down the street and introduced us to the local banker. Once he had his *poisson* on the line, he wasn't about to let it off the hook.

Mortgages are available for fifteen years or shorter terms; thirty-year mortgages do not exist in France. As in the United States, rates are fixed or variable, with a slight discount for the variable rates, which of course can go up or down. The current rate for a variable rate mortgage of fifteen years is about five-and-a-half percent. These rates apply to mortgages with ten percent down. You can put more down, of course. If paying ten percent down, you must pay compulsory mortgage insurance, which the bank supplies. This pays off the mortgage in the event the insured dies.

The process involved to get the mortgage approved is the same as in the United States, meaning that the bank will want details on your financial health, such as personal income tax returns or proof of other income.

The purchase is finalized with a *procuration* (final commitment), which can be signed in your notary's office. If you are finalizing the purchase from the United States, you can sign papers at the French embassy or consulate.

Le Notaire

A legal entity that you will hear mentioned over and over in France is the *notaire*. This person is a government official, who can advise both parties in home purchases. The *notaire* must ensure that the seller has a clear title to transfer, that money is transferred appropriately to the parties concerned, and that all taxes and registration fees are paid.

You can choose your own *notaire*, and the fees will be split between the two buyer and seller *notaires*. However, it's not necessary to have your own *notaire*, and you can share with the seller.

You can find a *notaire* by the signs hanging outside their offices or look in the yellow pages. If you want one who speaks English or has experience with foreign owners, ask for recommendations from other English speakers in the area, the local U.S. consulate, or a large local bank.

Taxes and Fees

Before purchasing a property in France, ask for a complete list of all taxes and fees involved. When you close on your house, you'll pay a tax based on the property's value and its age. A house built within the last five years is a "new" house if sold by the builder or the first buyer. In this case, the tax is two-and-a-half percent of the purchase price. If the property is more than five years old or has already been sold by the original buyer before, the tax varies depending on the area of the country, between six-and-a-half percent and eleven-and-a-half percent of the purchase price.

In most parts of France, the seller pays the real estate agent's fee; however in certain areas, it's the reverse. Again, ask for a complete summation.

At the closing you will pay for the property, the *notaire* fees, the stamp duty, and the land registration fees. The *notaire's* fees for the preparation of the *acte de vente* (including the TVA, France's value-added tax) are charged on a sliding scale, according to the purchase price of the property. The stamp duty (*enregistrement*) includes several taxes, which are recovered by the central, regional, and local governments.

As a rough guide, *notaire* fees, stamp duties, and other charges will be about twenty percent of the purchase price for a new house and about ten percent of the purchase price for an older house (because some fees are already in the purchase price). Consult a lawyer or tax expert to be sure you don't pay more stamp duty than necessary.

Land tax, or *taxe foncière*, is quite low. It is the estimate of the local rental value of the property. You do not have to pay this tax the first two years following the completion of a new building or the restoration of an old building.

Anyone who occupies a property in France, whether as owner or renter, pays a residential tax (*taxe d'habitation*). It's due on main and second homes.

La Viagère Lives!

Occasionally, you'll see the term *rente viagère* as a category of home sales. The *viagère* is a method by which a purchaser makes a low down payment on a property owned by an elderly person, then makes regular payments as long as the owner lives. The bet is that the owner will pass quickly.

But these people must all be descendants of Dorian Gray. One woman became the oldest woman in France, at 121, while the lawyer who purchased her house died of a heart attack, leaving his estate to continue paying for the home. Incidentally, French law says that the person holding the *viagère* cannot benefit from their "tenant's" untimely death, thus preventing countless murders by frustration.

10
Moving Crates and Critters

WHAT AFFECTS MEN SHARPLY ABOUT A FOREIGN NATION IS
NOT SO MUCH FINDING OR NOT FINDING FAMILIAR THINGS;
IT IS RATHER NOT FINDING THEM IN THE FAMILIAR PLACE.
—G. K. Chesterton

Moving your belongings to France is not much different from moving within the United States, except that your possessions enjoy an ocean cruise before reaching you.

France permits you to bring the normal contents of your apartment or home free of import duty, as long as you've owned those belongings for at least six months. This helps prevent enterprising souls from sneaking in items for the express purpose of becoming freelance importers. If you happen to tuck in a few new towels or pots and pans for your personal use, take the labels off.

Regulations permit Americans to bring 400 cigarettes, 100 cigars, or 500 grams of pipe tobacco duty free. You are allowed to bring two used cameras, ten rolls of film, and a movie camera with ten reels of film. I didn't know of the latter regulation and, in all innocence, packed my dad's collection of six vintage cameras. I don't know what they would have done if anyone had bothered to notice.

Do not pack guns or other weapons without having the proper permits from the consulate. Ammunition is prohibited, due to the risk of explosion on board the ship or plane.

House plants, seeds, or bulbs cannot be shipped to France without permission, because of the risk of importing nasty critters along with them.

What to Leave Behind

Televisions run on the French PAL/SECAM system in Europe, as opposed to the NTSC system used in the United States, so your television won't work here. You'll have to buy a French version. You'll also need an antenna for reception, though a satellite dish will improve reception considerably and expand the programs available. With a satellite dish, you'll have options for CNBC, BBC, TNT, CNN, and other English-language programming. Many of these are available off the air and do not require a monthly fee. Special satellite and cable packages with movie channels are available for a monthly charge.

VCRs will work with your current videocassettes, but not with the European standard, which is a different system. You can buy a VCR that plays both types. Specify that it be 220 volts for PAL/SECAM and is able to read NTSC.

As I mention in chapter 14, "Drive-It-Yourself" (see page 109), I don't recommend bringing a car to France. It's a hassle to adapt it to French regulations. It's much easier to sell it in the States and buy a new or good used car in France.

> We booked our tickets [to France] but our moods see-sawed,
> especially when we were tired of packing and sifting through belongings
> to move. But whenever we wondered if we were doing the right thing,
> we'd think about continuing in the same old rut.
> That prospect would always galvanize us.
> —Betsy and John, the Dordogne

MAKING THE MOVE PERMANENT

If you're moving permanently to France, find a moving company that's experienced in international moves. Call several movers and request estimates, then compare the size container you'll need and the cost. The representative will check your belongings to see what you plan to move and estimate the cost of labor and packing materials.

Note that the moving estimate is not always binding. The final bill depends on the actual weight of the load, which determines the packing charges. However, you will have a good idea of what the weight of the load is based on the volume of the container that's required.

When you have the estimates, call your local Better Business Bureau and Consumer Protection Agency to see if the mover has a good reputation. In comparing the estimates, check that the movers are supplying the same services and insurance. Some movers may try to get your business by estimating low, then bump the price with add-ons, so make sure everything is included. Check that they've included an appropriate quantity of packing materials if you're using their packers. Also, see how many movers they plan to use. A smaller crew may look less expensive, but if it takes more time, it will end up costing more in both money and frustration.

Check the insurance coverage provided by the mover. This is often inadequate, and at the last minute you may discover your belongings aren't properly covered unless you buy the optional extra insurance. When comparing estimates, know exactly which belongings are insured and how much the insurance will cover if these items are damaged.

International movers usually request payment in full before they will ship your belongings. Find out in advance if the company requires payment with a cashier's check, so you can have it ready.

Packing Up

If you're cutting costs, you can pack yourself, but it's not recommended. Considering the handling that your belongings will undergo in the sea voyage, you'd have to use professional methods, which most of us aren't accustomed to. Every item, including mattresses and box springs, will need to be packed in special cartons. Mirrors, artwork, and other fragile items should be crated or specially cushioned. Also, the moving company won't insure boxes you've packed.

An even better reason to have the mover do the packing is to ensure that your boxes will be marked "Mover Packed." This gives you an advantage in getting through customs smoothly on the other side of the pond. Apparently the customs authorities assume that movers avoid packing their clients' armaments and cocaine.

> We moved some of our belongings, but [after a bad experience
> moving in the States] we kept our house as security more than anything.
> My brother lives in the house and keeps our two dogs.
> —Amanda, Paris

Moving Containers

Metal ships' containers are transported by truck or rail to the port, where they are loaded onto a ship for the closest seaport, then reloaded onto a truck overseas and delivered. These containers are especially designed to offer protection against the elements on the ship's crossing.

Ship's containers come in standard sizes of twenty or forty feet. A 20-foot container holds approximately 1,100 cubic feet, which translates to about 8,000 pounds, or enough for the belongings for an apartment or small three-bedroom house. The forty-foot container, of course, holds double that. If you have a large home or want a car shipped, you'll need the larger size. The cost for a twenty-foot container from the East Coast of the United States is approximately $7,500; a forty-foot container is about $8,500, depending on weight and shipping locations.

Wooden lift crates are used for smaller shipments of about 200 cubic feet, normally under 4,000 pounds. You may share a ship's container with another person, though your possessions will be packed in separate crates. Sharing a container load can cut your costs of shipping considerably, although you'll have to be flexible as to delivery date, since the partial container may have to wait days or even weeks to be completed.

Smaller parcels can be sent via air, in special corrugated cardboard containers ranging from five to one hundred cubic feet.

International Moving Companies

Movers are listed in the yellow pages. Below are some of the larger international moving companies, with toll-free numbers and/or websites that provide information on moving services to France.

United Van Lines, Inc. Located at One United Drive, Fenton, MO 63026; telephone: (800) 325-3870.

Allied Van Lines. Website: *http://www.alliedvan.net.* This website will help you find local agents. It also provides tips on moving.

North American Van Lines. Website: *http://navl1.com.* As with most international movers, this company relies on local agents so see your yellow pages.

Vanpac International. Located at 1340 Arnold Drive, Suite 231, Martinez, CA 94553-4189; telephone: (800) 877-0444; e-mail: *sales@vanpac.com;* website: *http://www.vanpac.com.*

CUSTOMS ON ARRIVAL

When your goods begin their voyage, have the moving agent provide you with contact information for the agent in France. While your belongings travel, contact this agent to make sure the company has your correct address and phone number in France and can let you know as soon as your shipment arrives. The agent can also give you an estimated arrival date at the port, though they won't be able to tell you the exact delivery date at your house until the shipment has already cleared customs.

Contact the company in France well in advance of the estimated arrival date. The agent must have time to send you forms, which you are required to complete and return. Fill out and return these forms immediately, because they are needed to get your shipment through customs. It's up to you to ensure that customs arrangements have been made properly at the destination, thus avoiding costly storage fees, which are not included in your mover's fee.

We always assumed we'd bring Pumpkin, our 10-year-old cat, with us.
In fact, our plans to bring her finally convinced skeptical friends and
relatives that we really were serious about this.
—Betsy, the Dordogne

Bringing Pets

Four-footed friends are warmly welcomed in France, as long as they are healthy, have the required forms, and are older than three months old. Contact the French embassy or consulate for complete instructions on importing pets. Follow regulations and get the certificate that warrants your pet is disease-free. You will also need to show a certificate of vaccination for the usual diseases, including rabies, feline distemper, and leukemia. Some shots must have been given more than a month, but less than a year, before travel, so mark these dates on your moving calendar. Also, double-check the regulations, since they can change.

In the plane, your animal will travel in a specially climatized cargo area or, if small enough, may travel with you in the cabin. In the latter case, you must have an approved carrier and reserve space for the pet when you make your own reservations. The pet charge is approximately $100 one way. Ask the airline for any specific requirements.

When you arrive in France, find a good veterinarian and get a *Livret International de Santé* to list all your pet's health information. The required shots are basically the same as in the United States. Rabies vaccination is obligatory, and you must show proof of it to leave your pet in a kennel or to take it to a campground. Flea control pills, heart medicine, and other pet-care products are all available for your four-footed buddy.

France has a system of *tatouage* for dogs and cats. *Tatouage* is a numerical tattoo on the inside of the ear, which provides identification for rabies control and if the pet is lost. There's a national number to call if your pet is lost, which matches found pets with their numbers.

If you want to travel, France is a dream for your dog. They're accepted most places, including bars, cafés, and motels/hotels, though, in the case of motels/hotels, it's best to ask before you reserve. Grocery stores and fine restaurants will say "*non*" to animals. Museums and *châteaux* usually do not permit them, either, though some allow a pet if it's small and held in your arms during the visit.

If you choose to leave your pet while you travel within France, find a friend to pet-sit or a good kennel, which is called a *chenil.* You can request a free brochure published by a pet-food company, which lists more than 300 kennels in France by *département*. It shows addresses, hours, and services offered; although written in French, the listings use easy-to-understand symbols. For your copy, call toll-free (in France) 0800 41 51 61, and ask for *Le Guide Pratique Royal Canin*. Be prepared to give your name and address in France, and they'll mail it to you.

11
Chez Vous

LET YOUR BOAT OF LIFE BE LIGHT, PACKED WITH ONLY WHAT
YOU NEED—A HOMELY HOME AND SIMPLE PLEASURES....
—Jerome Klapka Jerome (1859–1927)

Finding a set of French stone walls to call your own makes you feel at home
in spirit, if not always in immediate comfort. Your French home will be
charming, solidly constructed—and filled with space that must be furnished. One can't live on French bread alone, and you'll soon begin accu-
mulating those things required of everyday life—bed and table and
something to cook on, as well as some unexpected items.

THE EMPTY-HOUSE SYNDROME

As mentioned before, unfurnished apartments and homes in France are
even emptier than most Americans expect. Unless agreed upon in the rental
or purchase contract, appliances and light fixtures, cupboards, shelves, and,
yes, even toilet-paper holders are likely to be missing in action. One
American even discovered, to his chagrin, that the previous owner had
absconded with the doorknobs.

Such perfidy isn't usual, though it does happen. Our house was in better shape than most. Though missing towel racks, we were left with the
satellite dishes, so we had a selection of TV channels to watch while resting
our sore feet after searching stores. (Towel racks and light fixtures had to fit
exactly if we didn't want additional holes in the walls.)

Check before Shopping

French rooms are tight on space, so measure the area available for furniture and appliances precisely. This means to the centimeter. Get a good tape measure with metric measurements. Don't rely on converting to inches. This only gives you a headache and eventually you'll give up and get a metric measure anyway. If you measure in metric, it's that much easier to match what you need to the sizes shown in the store.

Note in which direction doors, for example, on a washing machine or refrigerator, should open. Again, in tight spaces, this makes a world of difference.

Determine the type and location of water or electrical access and drainage. Consider the cost of electricity in your home, with particular notice to the discount you get if you use electricity during the off-peak hours. This will help you decide if you'd want programmable timers on the washer, dryer, or dishwasher in order to profit from the ability to start appliances after midnight—even if you're snoring soundly in bed.

A Note on Prices

Where I could, I've provided sample prices for various appliances and furnishings. These vary widely depending on the quality and number of features on the specific product. These prices are for new products. You may be able to find used furniture or appliances through classifieds or at a *dépôt vente* (used furniture) outlet. However, I've found that prices for used goods aren't all that wonderful. The French culture, unlike American culture, doesn't put as high a value on shiny new things, so the old goods don't fall in value as dramatically.

Appliances

If your housing does not include appliances, you will either eat out every meal or set up a kitchen. At the appliance store, you are in for a rude awakening because appliances in France often bear little in common with American ones, other than performing the same functions of cooling or heating or washing.

We spent far too much time trying to replicate American-style models in France. I'll review some of the differences, so that you'll know what's commonly available. Hopefully you'll learn from our mistakes and proceed with the business of selecting appliances based on those that are actually found in France, not what you think should be there.

Cook Top (Cuisinière)

To cook that flavorful French onion soup, you'll need a cook top. These are the closest to any U.S. appliance you'll find in France, since you'll have a choice of gas or electric burners. Even better, you can choose gas *and* electric. A combination of two of each type (or three gas and one electric) is common in this land of savvy cooks. The gas burners provide fast heating and are easily adjustable. These are also handy during expensive "red" electric days when costs skyrocket. (See chapter 12, "Warmth, Water, and All That Garbage.") The electric burners on the cook top provide an easier way to slowly simmer soups and stews, which is difficult to regulate on a gas flame, especially as you enjoy the breeze blowing in an open window.

The gas can come from the city or town supply, or your cook top may be adapted to use bottled gas bought at the local gas station or supermarket. You pay a bottle deposit then lug the thing home. One bottle lasts a long time (ours went a year) and, yes, we did make more than reservations for dinner. You may want to keep an extra bottle outside, if you have a safe place to store it, in case you run out just as the dinner party is about to commence.

Le Bon Mot: Major & Small Appliances

Congélateur	Freezer
Cuisinière	Cook top
Fer à repasser	Iron
Four	Oven
Lave-vaisselle	Dishwasher
Machine à laver	Washing machine
Micro-onde	Microwave
Réfrigérateur	Refrigerator
Sèche-cheveux	Hair dryer
Sèche-linge	Clothes dryer

Oven (Four)

The numbers on a French oven dial bear no relationship to those on an American one. French ovens usually have numbers 1 through 9, which translate to various centigrade/Fahrenheit temperatures. See the cooking information on page 68. Due to variations, however, you'll have to experiment with favorite recipes to see how your oven heats. An oven thermometer will help you gauge if it's a "hot" or "cool" oven.

Self-cleaning ovens are available; so if you don't want to spend your time scrubbing burnt-on grease, check to see that the model you buy has this feature. Ovens range from the most basic models to option-stuffed styles, with prices approximately 2500 to 6000 FF or about $416 to $1,000.

Microwave Oven (Micro-onde)

You can purchase a microwave oven that's simply a microwave, or one that combines a traditional oven, grill, and microwave. Prices range from 1500 to 3000 FF or about $250 to $500.

Refrigerator (Réfrigérateur)

The typical French refrigerator is a midget compared to American versions, because kitchens are smaller in France and people tend to buy food as needed, often every day.

Some styles include a freezer compartment, which come in various sizes and shapes. Side-by-side models, which are large, are the most expensive. Automatic defrost is available. When you look at the labels on refrigerators at the store, check for the energy use, which will be shown on a scale of A to G. Just remember that A is A-okay and is G is a *gourmand* eater-of-energy.

Refrigerators range from about 2500 FF to over 7000 FF or from about $415 to more than $1,150.

Freezer (Congélateur)

Freezer units are available, if you have the room or desire for one, though I admit that I'm prejudiced against them, considering the fun and tastiness of daily fresh foods in France. However, if you want one they come in table top and larger styles. They come in tall and narrow styles with pull-out bins, or a horizontal, trunk style. Prices range from 2000 FF (about $333) for the smallest to 4000 FF ($667).

Dishwasher (Lave-Vaisselle)

Dishwashers aren't especially common in France, due to the high cost of energy and the small kitchen space. They work basically the same as machines you're accustomed to, except they heat their own water. Some models are equipped with timers, so you can set it for washing in the wee hours when electric rates fall. Prices range from 3500 FF to 6000 FF or about $583 to $1,000.

Washing Machine (Lave-Linge)

Most European washing machines open at the top, rather than the front (though these are available), and have a tumble system that looks like a hamster treadmill. You lift the top lid, then open a metal door inside.

French machines work well, but they take at least an hour—often much longer if you want hot water—to wash anything. Five-kilo machines are standard, so giant loads are out of the question. A six-kilo machine is rare, but does exist, if you have the space and are willing to part with more francs.

When purchasing, check that the machine has a good spin (*essorage*) cycle. These can usually be regulated if you don't want a spin cycle at all (for delicates, for example), but you should have the possibility of a spin cycle that goes at least 800 cycles per minute or more. The higher the spin cycle, the more water is removed from the clothes. This is essential if you plan on using a dryer, since otherwise the electric cost will spin your budget out of control. Washers run from about 2300 FF ($383) for a simple machine to 3700 FF ($617). The larger, six-kilo size is the most expensive at 5200 FF or more ($867 and up).

Clothes Dryer (Sèche-linge)

Dryers are not as common in France as in the United States, due to lack of space and the fact that they gobble up that precious commodity, electricity, merely to dry clothes—and everyone in Europe knows that's what the sun and breeze outside are for. Nonetheless, I'll admit it was a blessed day when I got mine. After three weeks of solid rain, we were running short of clothes. Most French solve this by having a spot somewhere in the house where they hang clothes, when the balcony or backyard is too wet. On cold damp days, if there's a spot in front of the fireplace or a radiator, so much the better.

If you decide on a dryer, there are two kinds. The most common type evacuates the water removed from the clothes as hot, moist air, which is blown outside. The second type is a condensation dryer, which condenses the hot moist air and collects the resulting water in a bin inside the machine. You empty this (and a lint filter) after each load. In stone houses, the condensation dryer solves the problem of not having access to an out-side wall or vent. All you need is the electric outlet. If you want to convert a condensation dryer to eliminate the water via a tube to a sink, you can purchase a kit for this purpose.

Dryer prices range from 2000 FF to 4500 FF (about $333 to $750). For equivalent features, the condensation type costs more than the direct-evac-uation style.

Combination Washer/Dryer (Lavante-séchante)

Space-saving combination units wash the requisite 5 kilos of clothes, but dry only half that amount (2.5 kilos), since the dryer needs spin room to fluff out the clothes. For this reason the combination units are recom-mended only for a maximum of one person or a couple. They're expensive, at about 6000 FF or about $1,000.

Note that some regular dryers will stack on top of their matching wash-ers. If you have a space problem, check into this as a space-saving option that will provide the full five-kilo drying capabilities instead of the half capacity of the combination units.

"Sun-Powered" Drying

On Paris balconies and country courtyards, you'll see lines swaying with towels, shirts, and underwear. This is not considered a blight, as it is in the

United States, where suburban neighborhoods forbid the pleasure of fresh sun-dried clothes. In France it's often a necessity! Hang dryers (*sechoirs*) are found in general merchandise, hardware, and large grocery stores. They beat the high cost of electric drying, though it helps to have a sheltered spot in case of rain.

No Laundry Space?

If you don't have room for washing and/or drying, your options are hand wash, laundromat, or professional cleaners. In Paris you can find laundomats, but they're rare in small country towns.

Even if you have a washing machine at home, it won't hold anything bigger than five kilos worth (about ten pounds), so you'll still need a laundry for blankets or drapes. Bring lots of coins.

Commercial laundry services (*blanchisserie*) and dry cleaners (*nettoyage à sec*) are readily available but expensive compared to U.S. prices. Resign yourself to leaving the items for several days. Rarely will you get next-day service.

In the winter, we put our wash in front of the fireplace before we go to bed. In the morning they're nicely dried just from the remaining heat.
—Christine, Loire Valley

Furnishings

The sofas, chairs, bedding, desks, and other such items that make your home comfortable are available in France in a wide range of options, from cheap plywood to elaborate and beautiful antiques to contemporary decorator items.

For most people moving here, the pleasurable way to furnish a home is by wandering the antique markets (*brocantes*) for period pieces—or even just used furniture that you can adapt with paint or stencils. Attractive, middle-of-the-road items, meaning those that aren't ready to fall apart but aren't in the price range of Versailles, are often the most difficult to find. For inexpensive furnishings and accessories, try chain stores, such as Conforama, Ikea, Fly, or Sesame.

If you're moving permanently to France, you can bring your furniture with you. Even if the moving fee is steep, it may be the less expensive route if you would otherwise have to buy a lot of furnishings.

Our frustrations are little ones, like learning to buy the right things.
Lamps here have two or three types of sockets and electrical cords have myriad
plug styles. Naturally, on the first go-round, we invariably buy the one that
doesn't match. The result is returning for endless exchanges.

—Betsy, the Dordogne

Storage

Closets are smaller in France than in the States—if accommodations are equipped with them at all. New homes will have closets built in, though again, they are smaller than what Americans are accustomed to. Older homes may have no built-in closets. This is why those marvelous *armoires* were built. Thus, consider when you rent or buy that you may have to invest in something, if only egg crates, in which to store shirts and sweaters.

Textiles

For some unfathomable reason, linens, towels, and such are costly in France. If you move your belongings, bring them. Towels are scrawny things in France that still cost more than in the States. I complained about their anorexia, until I realized that the thinness made it easier to wash more than two of them in the small French washing machines. Which came first? The small machines or the small towels?

If you import your own beds, be sure to bring the sheets to fit them. Mattresses are a different size in France. You might be able to manage with flat sheets by tucking them in or resigning yourself to having them be a bit sloppy. Queen-size sheets are a tad big but will do for a French-size double mattress.

Curtains and draperies are reasonable. You can purchase shades and blinds reasonably if the standard sizes fit your windows, or you can special order them. Remember that French windows open inwards from the center. Blinds and shades must attach to each side separately or be set above the window frame, so you can pull the blinds out of the way before opening the window.

I wanted my sofa cleaned, but it's not like the States. I had to call
the insurance agent, who recommended a specialist. He took it outside
and washed it and left it there to dry.
We couldn't sit on it for two days.

—Pam, Le Mans

Miscellania

All those extra gadgets, such as towel racks that you can pop into any Wal-Mart for in America are found in France, just not in great variety. You'll undoubtedly do more shopping if you're at all fussy about style or shape. Auchan and Continent are large chain stores that carry a variety of household items. Some common kitchen items are also found in the supermarkets.

Small appliances can be more expensive in France than the States. Shop around. Bring your own small appliances from the U.S. if you want, but plan to use an adapter plug and the appropriate converter or transformer to switch the voltage from the U.S. 110 to France's 220. For more information on electrical adapters, converters, and transformers, see page 96.

Le Bon Mot: Furnishings

Armoire	Wardrobe cupboard
Canapé	Inedible. It's a sofa.
Chaise	Straight chair
Commode	Nope, not that. It's a chest of drawers.
Fauteuil	Armchair
Lit	Bed
Matelas	Mattress
Meubles	Furniture in general
Moquette	Wall-to-wall carpet
Sommier	Box spring
Table	Yes, it means table.
Tapis	Rug

Repair Services

Lawns and houses need repairs in France just as they do anywhere else. You will be dealing with various services. This is another reason to start making friends with local people as soon as possible. In France, more than the United States, services are delivered on a personal basis. You will not necessarily get better service if you offer more money. I tried that when we first moved into a rented house. The electricity went out on a Friday evening, just before a long, potentially lightless, weekend. I phoned several servicemen but, unlike in the States where overtime leads to early retirement, none of them were eager to get my business. Not even when I specifically asked about holiday charges.

Fortunately, the farm wife next door knew the trick to fixing it. We learned from the experience. Since then friends have recommended plumbers and electricians and other service people, whom we've used regularly. We now know that "our" servicemen will show up.

Well, most of the time.

Below are various household servicepeople and their main responsibilities in France.

Ebéniste	Cabinetmaker	Makes and installs fitted cabinetry and furniture.
Electricien	Electrician	Fixes electrical problems. Installs lighting fixtures. Repairs electric ranges, electrical heating (if the problem is electrical, but not radiators), and electric water heaters.
Menuisier	Woodworker	Works with and fixes windows, doors, staircases, trim, in both wood and PVC.
Plombier	Plumber	Works on water pipes, but also repairs heating systems involving radiators and fuel oil.
Ramoneur	Chimney Sweep	Inspects and cleans chimneys; an annual requirement for your home insurance.

Use your local artisan. Our experience with French workers is
a) they do high-class, efficient work for reasonable (that is to say, honest) prices;
b) you want to support your local economy; c) it's good for your French; and
d) the English guy with whom you can communicate so easily may be okay,
but he also may be a rip-off artist whose forté is being able to speak English.

—Margot, Drôme Provençale

12
Warmth, Water, and All That Garbage

The plumbing, heating, and electrical systems in France are an exciting mystery to be solved, especially if you purchase an older home. Our home, at 150 years of age, has been modernized, though wires and tubes create a maze of trails to be followed.

Even with a new house or small apartment, whether you rent or purchase, requires you to deal with utility companies. For the most part this is a straightforward process. Any number of people can lead you to the right suppliers for your location—your rental agent, landlord, real estate agent, or previous owner. In our case, the owner provided a list of the local companies, including three fuel suppliers for our crotchety old furnace. If possible, request such a list. It will be a tremendous help.

UTILITY *PRÉLEVEMENTS*

Virtually every utility in France will debit the bills directly from your bank account. When you sign up for service, take the details on your account in the form of a *rélevé d'identité bancaire,* called a *rib* for short. These forms are located in the back of your checkbook, or you can request extras from your bank. (For more information on *prélevements,* see chapter 16.)

Electricity

The electrical current in France is 220 volts, 50 cycles versus the U.S. 110 volts, 60 cycles. In addition, the plugs (*prises*) are an entirely different shape. To use electrical appliances purchased in the United States, you'll need adapters and converters or transformers.

The adapter plug does absolutely nothing to modify electricity. It merely provides a means by which you can put your American flat-pronged plug into the round European-shaped socket.

A converter can convert power for an electric appliance (for example, from 110 to 220 volts). Converters will work for short-term, high-voltage use on simple appliances, such as hair dryers, vacuum cleaners, coffee makers, and so on. As a general rule, they work for appliances that don't have to be kept plugged in regularly. Check the manufacturer or supplier of the converter for recommendations.

Do *not* use a converter with any electronic appliances (those containing microchips). This can mean even the most mundane products these days, so be sure to check. Anything with an electronic component requires a transformer.

A transformer converts the power supply, enabling you to use electronic appliances, such as computers, copiers, or fax machines. A transformer works with either electric or electronic products, so if you're unsure, choose the transformer over a converter. Buy the proper size transformer, based on the wattage of the appliance. Check with the manufacturer of the transformer to see which one will work with the relevant electronic appliance.

In the United States, you can purchase adapters, converters, and transformers at travel stores and electronic shops, such as Radio Shack, or through catalogs, such as Franzus (203-723-6664); Magellan's (800-962-4943; or Walkabout Travel Gear (800-274-4277) or check their website at *http://www.walkabouttravelgear.com/wwelect.htm* for reams of useful information.

In France you can find adapters, converters, and transformers at hardware stores and large general merchandise stores.

Cutting Costs

The French actually *do* what our American mothers nagged us about: They shut off lights when they leave the room. In the case of hotel hallways, sometimes they even shut off the lights *before* you leave the room, if the timers run out on you. Paying your own electricity bill means you'll soon join them in learning to save power.

Electricité de France (EDF) is state-owned and supplies the power for most of the country. Electricity in France is largely supplied via nuclear plants, and the country produces it inexpensively and sells it to much of Western Europe. This, however, does not make the electricity cheap for the consumer.

EDF offers various plans for home service. As soon as you know the date you'll move in, apply at the local EDF office for connection to set up the service plan you prefer. You will be asked to show an attestation that you're the owner or have a lease, plus your passport or residence permit (*carte de séjour*).

The price is based on the amount of power supplied to the house. You will have a choice of the normal rate, which charges the same for electricity twenty-four hours a day. You can also pick a reduced-rate system in which you have a lower rate at night, when you will heat hot water. (EDF or an electrician can install the necessary relays.) Your meter and bill will separate the day and night use.

A system called *Tempo* encourages conservation on winter days when demand is highest and France sells its power to other countries. (They want you to cut use, so they can sell more of it.) It's based on a six-tiered pricing system. Basically, there are three colors of days (patriotically colored blue, white, and red) each of which is further subdivided into the times when electricity is most popular (*heures pleines*) and the times when it's not (*heures creuses*). On blue and white days, the cheapest hours are between 10 p.m. and 6 a.m. On red days, the cheapest times are between midnight and 6 a.m.

There are twenty-two red days in which electricity is almost ten times more costly than the full "blue" rate. Red days occur only between November 1 and March 31, except for holidays and weekends. The idea is to avoid using energy guzzlers, such as electric heat, washer, dryer, dishwasher, oven, and halogen lights on red days, though moderate use of other lights and television or radio are fine. There are also forty-three "white" days each year, in which the cost of power is double that of blue days.

If you can arrange your schedule to avoid the most expensive times, using electricity for the most part on blue days, then theoretically, you'll cut your electric bill. I say theoretically because red days always seem to occur on American Thanksgiving (not a holiday in France), just when we want the oven for turkey and pies that will take exactly seven hours and twenty-seven minutes of the most expensive hours on the planet.

If you opt for the Tempo system, EDF provides you with a personal nag in the form of a small electronic monitor the size of an oven timer, which lights up after 8 p.m. showing you the "color" of the next day. This, of course, will set off a frantic effort to do three loads of wash before the jig is up.

Whichever system you choose is up to you, depending on your flexibility and willingness to make the effort.

The electric bill (*facture*) arrives every two months. It can be paid by direct debit (*prélèvement*) from your bank account.

Le Bon Mot: Utilities

Abonnement . . . . Subscription
À payer avant . . . . To be paid before (date)
Compteur . . . . Meter
Consommation . . . . Consumption
Facturation . . . . Invoicing
Facture . . . . Bill
Frais . . . . Expenses/costs
Hors taxe. . . . . Tax free
Montant . . . . Sum/total
Prix. . . . . Price
Redevance . . . . Rental fee
Taxe . . . . Tax

Heating Systems

France generates electricity primarily from nuclear power, and electricity is often used for heating. Natural gas is supplied by *Gaz de France* (GDF) and is available in towns and cities that already have the infrastructure in place—probably not in your farmhouse in the country.

In the countryside, you're more likely to see the humped-whale shapes of fuel tanks; some homes have oil tanks in their cellar areas. Fuel is pronounced the same as in English, though it's spelled *fioul* in French. You order fuel by the liter from a local supplier, who pumps it into the tank. A gauge tells you how much fuel remains so you can see when it's time to reorder.

Other forms of heating include old fireplace-fueled hot water systems—use this system only if you enjoy building fires in the dead of night to keep radiators warm.

Our central heating works fine, except in our large schoolroom
[converted into a home], which is over 200 cubic meters. It was barely warm
and using a tank of gas per month, to the tune of around 4500 FF ($750).
So we bought the beautiful, traditional Godin stove and now
burn wood....What a savings!

—Margo, Rémuzat

WATER

Tap water is safe to drink in France. It's supplied by *Générale des Eaux*, though mineral content will be different in every area, depending on the local subsidiary. If you prefer, spring water is sold in supermarkets and *les épiceries*. You can also buy water filters.

Water is billed once a year. After the first year, you can make arrangements to pay in installments.

In farm areas you may have a well or spring. This is a source of concern for two reasons: safety and supply. If you have well water, have it analyzed by the public health department or water authority. In the south particularly, wells are subject to drought, so make sure that the water supply will be regular.

Water that's drinkable is *potable*. If it's unsafe, it's marked *nonpotable*. You'll often see the latter written on town fountains and lavatories on trains, for example.

GARBAGE

Regularly scheduled garbage pickups are usual in most areas in France excepting the most remote. For large items, such as old carpet rolls or rusted-out appliances, you must take things to the *déchetterie*, or wait for a specific day when oversized things are picked up. You'll see notices posted or listed in a town newsletter, or you can ask at your local town hall.

The *déchetterie* is also the place where you recycle plastic and glass, old oil from your car, and garden detritus. For plastic and glass bottles, recycling bins are located in areas around town, often outside supermarkets. Look for bright green kiosks with round holes through which you push the bottles.

13
Training and Other Big Wheels

RESTORE HUMAN LEGS AS A MEANS OF TRAVEL. PEDESTRIANS RELY ON
FOOD FOR FUEL AND NEED NO SPECIAL PARKING FACILITIES.
—Lewis Mumford

Americans consider a car's gas pedal to be an appendage of the foot. This is
not as true in France, where public transportation is more accessible and
more readily adopted by the general public.

The *Métro* in Paris and the train system that treks across the country
are a joy, whisking you through the countryside, avoiding standstill city
traffic, and letting you read, nap, or enjoy the scenery, instead of hunching
over a wheel.

Unless, of course, there's a strike.

Then you're stranded and have to do as we did once when we
attempted to make an outward-bound flight. We planned extra hours in
advance, then dragged luggage and dog down dreary corridors, up stairs,
and down streets to make the necessary connections.

Le Métro

The most elaborate underground train system in France is the Paris *Métro*,
which covers the city in a system that's simple once you understand the
basics. First, get a map of the *Métro* at any *Métro* ticket booth and keep it in
your pocket. The various train lines are indicated by color. Check for the *end*
points of each of these lines. These tell you the direction you want to go.

Do not confuse the *Métro* with the RER (*Réseau Express Régional*), which is the suburban train network that also operates in the Paris area. They operate in different directions, though often you'll see signs for them in the same terminal.

> *Owning a car in Paris is like being attached to a ball and chain.*
> *Thanks to the best public transportation in the world,*
> *I am no longer a slave to a vehicle or the rules of the road!*
> *When I want to tour the countryside, I just rent [a car].*
> —Adrian, Paris

Trains

The *Société Nationale des Chemins de Fer* (SNCF) is France's country-wide rail network. It is state-owned and amazingly efficient and punctual. The train clerks in the small towns will go out of their way to solve your logistical transportation problems, if you hang in there and persist. (It's easier when there isn't a line of other potential passengers growing out the door behind you.) In Paris, I can't promise that you'll get the same attention as in small towns. Think of New York City, and you'll understand.

The good and bad news about the system is that SNCF uses Paris as a hub. This is convenient for Parisians. For everyone else it usually works, especially for most international rail travel in that direction. But sometimes you have to go through Paris, even if the crow would find a shorter route.

The *Train à Grand Vitesse* (TGV) is a special case. The TGV can travel at speeds of up to 300 kilometers (187 miles) an hour, yet feels like riding a magic silk carpet. It uses special tracks, so it does not go into every station, though it does cover much of the country.

Unlike regular trains, TGV trains require reserved seats. You must buy a ticket and sit in the designated place, so be sure to indicate smoking or nonsmoking, first or second class. The high speed train tracks also extend to some places outside France.

In Paris you can board trains that go directly to all the major European cities. Hop on one and be in Florence, Geneva, Madrid, Vienna, or Venice or any of hundreds of other destinations. You can even cross the channel to London.

Purchasing a Ticket

Tickets can be purchased from a clerk at a ticket window or from a machine (*billetterie automatique*) at all SNCF stations. Whether you're purchasing from a machine or a human, note that there are different tickets for main line TGV than for local trains. Get in the correct line. Some machines operate in different languages, enabling you to read in English, if you push the British button. The clue is a British flag.

Schedules are available at the train station, along with brochures (in French), explaining pricing and services.

You can purchase first- or second-class seating on French trains. The difference is negligible for comfort, especially if you travel by TGV, so it's usually not worth the additional cost. The TGV and regular trains are the same price for the same distance; however a reservation fee is charged for TGV trains.

Credit cards, such as Visa and MasterCard, can be used at the ticket window for purchases more than 100 FF (about $17).

Discounts

A variety of discounts are available for train tickets. Families, seniors, children, students, and commuters can get special deals. Special excursion pricing is available, if you stay overnight Saturday and Sunday. Note that there are different prices for different travel hours. The less popular (*bleu*) hours are the lowest priced. There's a discount for booking your ticket eight days in advance.

Additional discounts apply to children, students, and seniors with the purchase of a *carte* (card). For those who travel often, the savings pay for the card's cost. For example, any senior (60 or older) can requested a tariff called *Découverte Senior,* which offers a twenty-five percent discount on fares during the *bleu* periods. However, seniors who purchase a *Carte Senior* for 290 francs (about $49) are eligible for a year of discounts that cut fifty percent off the ticket for first- or second-class travel during the *bleu* travel periods and twenty-five percent off international train travel in over twenty participating countries.

Numerous subscription deals are available for users who commute regularly. Though SNCF is supposedly simplifying the pricing system, it's still complicated and changes often. My advice is to tell the clerk where you want to go and when, then ask for the lowest-priced ticket. When he tells you, ask again if that's the lowest price. Most of the time, he'll go back to the computer and come up with a better deal. I once stood there for fifty minutes, while he compared different combinations of days, times, stations, and discounts, to get me the best price. Fortunately, he wasn't busy and was determined to solve my "problem" of wanting the best deal.

This works best if the clerk's not harried by rush hour and a horde of customers, so if you're purchasing a major train ticket go at an off time and don't rush the process.

I also advise making friends with your local agent. I can't tell you the number of times our agent has bent the rules to get a better price (a round-trip price, for example, even though I was going to Roissy and returning from Paris), because I was "*une bonne cliente.*"

Compostez Your Ticket

Before boarding a train, always get your ticket stamped by one of the *composteur* machines located at the entrance to the platforms. They're painted bright orange and tell you to "*Compostez votre billet.*"

Insert the ticket in the machine, the ticket will be notched and imprinted. This validates it. If your ticket is not stamped when the conductor checks it, you can be fined at least 36 francs (about $6), or up to twenty percent of the fare.

You can stamp your ticket early. I do this when I arrive, even if I have to wait for hours, since then it's done. The stamped tickets can be used all day, so even if you miss a train, you can use it on the next one. If you stamp it, and you cancel your plans, or there are no more trains that day, go to the ticket window and have the clerk unvalidate the ticket so you can use it the next day.

If you ever do forget to get your ticket stamped, look pitiful, speak English, and say you didn't understand what you were supposed to do. It didn't work for me, but I saw it work with two little old ladies once.

LE BON MOT: NAVIGATING THE STATION

Billet	Ticket
Caisse	Cashier
Composteur	Stamping machine (for tickets)
Correspondance	A change of train lines
Gare	Station
Quai	Track
Sortie	Exit
Voiture	Train car

PARIS TRAIN STATIONS

Paris has six train stations, each of which is dedicated to serving a different area of the country and/or Europe. Your ticket will note the station. Stations and their main destinations are:

Gare d'Austerlitz	Southwest and central France, including the cities of Bordeaux and Toulouse—except for TGV service (see *Gare Montparnasse*); Portugal and Spain.
Gare de l'Est	East (Nancy, Strasbourg); Germany and East Europe.

Gare de Lyon	South and southeast, including the cities of Lyon and Marseilles, plus the Cote d'Azur area, TGV southeast routes; Switzerland, Italy, and Greece.
Gare Montparnasse	Western France (Brittany); TGV Atlantic routes including Bordeaux.
Gare du Nord	Northern France, including TGV service to Lille and London; Northern European areas, including Belgium, Holland, and the Scandinavian countries.
Gare St. Lazare	Northwest France, including Normandy.

Buses

Some French cities provide excellent bus services within their metropolitan area. If there is a city bus system, look for stops that say *l'autobus*.

In small towns and country areas, buses are used for school children, but are unavailable or impractical as a regular transportation system.

Long-distance tour buses are called *l'autocars*. These vehicles, unlike local buses, provide plush seats and toilet facilities on board. Some even offer video service and snacks. It should be noted that French law requires bus drivers to stop regularly for breaks, especially the long lunch, which is sacred. With all the stops, you'll be taking a longer trip than if you had driven. On the other hand, the breaks are a welcome chance to stand up and walk around and use facilities that aren't swaying over the *autoroute*.

Several companies, such as EuroLines, promote their bus services for travel on regularly scheduled voyages or as charter tours within France or to nearby countries. Bus tickets are generally less expensive than a comparable trip by train or air. But, of course, you'll be on the road much longer.

Ferries

Did you know that you can drive to Ireland from France? Just pull your car onto one of the passenger-and-car ferries, which provide regular services to various ports in Great Britain and Ireland. The number of crossings available at any one time depend on the popularity of the route (Dover/Calais is the shortest crossing, hence the most popular) and the season (winter crossings may be limited or nonexistent in some areas).

If traveling to Ireland, for example, you can take the car ferry overnight. A cabin lets you attempt sleep, unless you have two giggly teenage girls next door who've had a bit too much stout. (The walls are paper thin.)

From France, ferry services are most common from Le Havre, Roscoff, Calais, and Cherbourg, though other ports are available. Irish Ferries, Brittany Ferries, P&O, and Condor are a few of the ferry companies.

The Hovercraft makes the trip to Great Britain faster than the regular ferry service. The downside is that it's more expensive and, in choppy weather, your ticket will be useless because it won't go. This is one case where the Hovercraft is the rabbit but the ferry is the turtle, slow and sure.

> *When my cousin wanted to [meet us to] ski, the cost round-trip to Chamonix was cheaper than meeting in Denver. Even took less time. He flew Washington to Geneva direct.*
>
> —Cary, Pau

AIRLINES

Paris is the hub for major international flights, though flights are also available to Nice, Marseilles, and Lyon. Air France is the state-owned carrier, and developer of the Concorde, which makes a flight to New York City in three-and-a-half hours.

France's domestic airline is Air Inter. Its main competition are regional airlines and TGV service, since the TGV usually goes city center to city center. To reach Air Inter, contact Air France, 232, rue de Rivoli, 75001 Paris; telephone: 01 45 39 25 25, or any other Air France office.

A HINT ON TRAVEL DEALS FROM LONDON

If you plan to take some exotic vacations while based in France, consider shopping for tickets and tours via London. "Bucket shops" in London offer plane fares and vacation packages that are quite cheap, even if you add in the extra cost of taking the ferry or Chunnel to London.

SCHEDULING

Train, bus, and airline schedules in France run on the twenty-four-hour clock. The military is already accustomed to using this system. For the rest of us it takes adjustment but is a practical and simple way to tell morning from evening hours. After noon, the hours continue in the sequence so 1:00 p.m. is 13:00, 2:00 p.m. is 14:00, and so forth. When you get past noon, just subtract twelve from the twenty-four-hour-clock time, and you'll know the standard clock time; alternatively, add 12 if you're making an evening trip. Until it becomes a habit, ensure that you don't accidentally reserve for a 5:00 a.m. train when you meant 5:00 p.m. or 17:00.

Tourist Agents

Tourist agencies, large and small, compete for your travel business. Many of them publish and/or promote plush books of packaged vacations, which are designed to entice you to travel out of France. They all seem like such terrific deals when you're not traveling across the ocean to get there.

Local clubs and cultural groups offer group rates on special holiday trips. Newcomer (*accueil*) groups and retirement clubs (*troisième age*), for example, plan regular trips. Even local banks get in the act, with an array of special tours offered to customers.

One very special reason to live in France is its convenient location in Western Europe. You might as well take advantage of it!

14
Drive-It-Yourself

CURSED IS HE THAT DOES NOT KNOW THE WIDTH OF HIS CAR.
—Christopher Driver, "An Alternative Commination"

Our eleven-year-old, slightly dented Citroën has chauffeured us faithfully through fieldstone villages, past hectares of top-heavy sunflowers—and to our local garage. We've become dear friends with the service manager and, especially, the cashier. However, we've still saved bundles, considering the cost of a new car—or the two of them we'd be needing for our old lifestyle in the States.

Many people living in France can actually do without a car. This is mainly the option for those who live in Paris. Several friends of mine simply rent a car when they want to leave town on a driving vacation.

Even those who live in the countryside find that a car is less a necessity than in the States. The majority of couples manage well by sharing one vehicle. This is possible, because most areas are well served by trains, buses, *Métro* stations—or shoe leather. However, if you've run away to enjoy traveling on a regular basis, you'll need a vehicle for daily shopping and vacation trips.

BUYING A CAR

You can purchase a new or used vehicle; however, buying a used one avoids that "new car" hit you take by driving anything out the showroom. Fortunately, France's system of *Contrôle Technique* (see below) takes much of the worry out of buying a used vehicle, especially when you don't understand the language well.

Many types of cars are available in France, but Citroën, Peugeot, and Renault are practical choices. The French dealer network extends throughout the country as well as to several of its neighbors. It's comforting to know that service and parts are readily available if you intend to travel widely. Of course, there are other popular cars, such as Volkswagen, BMW, Fiat, Mercedes, and Ford, along with British, Japanese, and Spanish makes. If you choose a more esoteric brand, check the availability of parts and services before you buy.

Contrôle Technique

It's relatively easy to purchase a good used car in France—or at least know what problems you're getting. An inspection called *Contrôle Technique* is required by law before any used car is sold. The *Contrôle Technique* is a physical exam for a used car, telling you where its arteries may be blocked or where arthritis is about to overtake the engine.

The inspection lists problems under two basic categories—those that are essential to your safety, and those that are just, well, there.

All essential safety problems must be repaired before the car is sold, and the seller must prove this has been done by returning the vehicle for another inspection. The nonessential repairs don't have to pass inspection, but they're listed on the report so the buyer can see at a glance the state of the vehicle.

THE DEUX CHEVAUX

That miniscule vehicle with a snipped-off rear-end that's puttering down the road in front of you is France's answer to cheap transportation. It's a *deux chevaux* (2CV for short), which was made by Citroën and is now collected by aficionados throughout the country.

Carte grise

Once you buy a car, new or used, you will need a registration, or *carte grise*. Apply for this at the local *mairie* or *hôtel de ville* in the town where you live or in the *préfecture de police* or town hall of your *arrondissement*. If you change addresses after you get the *carte*, you must apply for a new one; if you're moving to a different *département*, you'll also have to register your car again.

The dealer will issue the *carte grise* for a new car; when you buy a used car (*vehicule d'occasion*), take the paperwork to the appropriate authority yourself.

...And Putt-Putt Horsepower

Newer than the 2CV are some small puddle-jumpers whose closest kin seems to be a lawn mower engine. Their previous claim to fame was that they didn't require a driver's license, making it popular among people who couldn't get one or didn't want to spend $300 for the driver's lessons necessary to get the license. These micro-cars only go about 40 mph. Interesting, but you don't want one for touring.

Car Insurance

Car insurance is required in France for third-party medical costs and damage to property. You can apply for car insurance through your local bank or a private insurance company, such as Groupama or AXA.

Your premium will depend on the car and coverage you select. You can reduce the premium, if you opt for a deductible. The insurance sticker must be displayed on your windshield. Also, carry copies of the insurance forms with you in case of an accident.

Name That Department...

Is that elegant lady a Parisian? Check her license plate. The last two digits tell where the car is registered and are based on the number of the *département*. It's a great way to tell the tourists from the locals.

The Tax Vignette

Every year your vehicle must have a tax *vignette*, a sticker that shows you've paid your taxes. The amount due depends on the horsepower of your car, its age, and the department in which it's registered.

You must purchase your *vignette* at a *tabac* (tobacconist) by November 30 each year for the subsequent year and install it on the windshield by December 1. If you miss the deadline, you'll be fined an extra ten percent as a late payment and adding insult to injury, you will have to go to the nearest *préfecture* for it, instead of around the corner.

You're learning from our mistakes, because our first year, we didn't even realize there was such a thing as a *vignette*. Finally, a French friend mentioned it, but it was already two days after the deadline. We drove thirty-seven kilometers for what we could have done a block from our house. A word to the wiser...mark it on your calendar.

We brought our Honda Accord over but had terrible problems.
We assumed [the rules] would be the same as here [the U.S.]...
but the car needed to conform with headlights, this, and that.
I wouldn't advise bringing a car!

—Sara, the Ardèche

Le Bon Mot: Driving Legalities

Assurance	Insurance
Carte grise.	Registration
Contrat	Contract
Contrôle technique	Vehicle inspection
Devis.	Estimate (insurance or repairs)
Multirisque tous accidents/ . .	Comprehensive/
tous risque	all accidents (insurance coverage)
Permis de conduire	Driver's license
Vignette.	Registration sticker

Driver's License

You can drive in France on a valid U.S. driver's license until you're a resident. France requires full-time residents to have a French license.

For this, you need driving lessons. No, it doesn't matter if you've been driving since Ben Hur, the French assume you know nothing and believe you must take lessons. Costly lessons.

Currently the regulation is under study, but until the lesson requirement is changed, the only way around it is to trade a U.S. driver's license for a French one within nine months of arrival. Certain states have reciprocal agreements with France, among them are Florida, Illinois, Kansas, Kentucky, Michigan, New Hampshire, Pennsylvania, and South Carolina.

If your home in France is secondary and you do not plan to reside in France full-time, just keep your U.S. license.

En Route

Aside from village streets that are the width of a flea, roads in France are generally good. High-speed *autoroutes* charge tolls for the privilege of going 130 kilometers an hour (about 82 mph—and the French will be passing you in a blur) on a road with nothing more interesting to see than the next chain restaurant. These are just like expressways in the States, in that they make sense when you're heading from A to B for a long distance and need to make good time. They also offer regular rest stops, gasoline stations, and food options. For the speed and convenience, they can be worthwhile.

If you have time and want to see more of the country, try smaller roads. The national roads (*routes nationales*) are decent and frequently trail beside the *autoroutes*. They are often just two lanes, however, so beware of impatient French drivers. National roads go through towns, from time to time, so you'll be adjusting your speed accordingly. The good news is that, if you're not in a hurry, *routes nationales* provide a chance to see something other than just another *baguette/frites* stand along the *autoroute*.

Routes départmentales are smaller department roads. In terms of charm, they beat the *routes nationales*, since they allow you to lose yourself in one charming small town after another.

Many roads through small towns give Americans claustrophobia. The confined space between stone walls, with twists and turns and narrow one-way streets make a good case for a small car. Eventually you'll adjust and skim past the walls like the best French driver. After all, if those eighteen-wheelers bringing all those potatoes and tomatoes into town can make it, then so can you.

Breakdowns

If you experience a problem on the road, pull off and put on your emergency flashers. *Autoroutes* have breakdown lanes, and national routes have wider areas designed for this purpose—or for picnicking, which the French consider a greater necessity at midday.

Le Bon Mot: Filling Up

Essence	Gasoline
Sans plomb	Unleaded
Gasoil/gazole	Diesel
Libre service	Self-service
Plein	Full/fill it up
Plomb	Leaded

Rules of the Road

The French drive on the right, so Americans have a head start on the British here. Seat belts are required to be worn in all seats, front and back. *Les gendarmes* enforce this rule, as you'll see from their presence occasionally on the side of the road stopping drivers on holiday weekends.

Children under the age of ten must ride in the back unless they have an approved seat facing rearwards, or the car has no back seat. Children must use a safety belt or a car safety seat.

Despite their love of wine, the French have strict regulations against combining drinking with driving. *Les gendarmes* can check your condition with a breathalyzer test (*alcooltest/dépistage*) at random. If you're convicted of drunk driving, you can lose your license, face a heavy fine, and spend up to two years in prison. And your car insurance may not cover you any longer. Yes, this is another good reason to use public transportation or a designated driver after a night on the *ville.*

Stoplights

You'll recognize the stoplight as such; however you may not be able to tell yellow from red. The colors aren't as definitive as they are in the States, so watch carefully.

Stop at the light, even if it's twenty yards from the corner of the street...and don't creep. On the narrow old-world streets, cars and especially trucks need space to turn. The lights are strategically placed for this reason.

Right-turn-on-red is allowed only when specified.

Speed Limits

Autoroute speed limits are set at 130 kph (kilometers per hour), which is about 82 mph; in rain it lessens to 110 kph (69 mph). Limits will be reduced in mountain areas with steep curves or in work lanes.

The speed limit on national routes is usually 110/100 kph (69/62 mph), or 90/80 kph (56/50 mph). These routes are not divided highways, so be especially wary. Make sure you know who's coming up behind you and what's coming toward you. When it comes to passing at odd times, some French people seem to have a death wish. Make sure they don't take you with them.

In towns and populated areas, the speed automatically goes down to 50 kph (31 mph). Usually signs will show this reduction, but not always. You're expected to know that entering a town lowers the speed limit. When you see the town sign (rectangular with the name of the village or town), that should be your reminder to slow down.

For a full list of French driving regulations, get a copy of the French highway code (*Code de la Route*) at a bookstore or driving school.

Finding Your Way

A good map will help you plan your route in advance and avoid getting off track. Check the route to your final destination, then follow signs in the direction of towns along the way. It's like following bread crumbs: Just head for one town after another, until you reach your objective.

When leaving a town, you'll see signs to certain towns. If you're heading that way, follow the signs. Anything else is *autres directions* (other directions).

Le Bon Mot: Essential Signs

Stop.....................	Stop
Cédez le passage	Yield
Vous n'avez pas la priorité. . .	Yield
Sens unique..............	One way
Sens interdit	Do not enter
Stationnement interdit	No parking
Serrez à droite/gauche......	Stay to the right/left
Allumez vos feux/phares	Turn on your lights
Attention travaux	Careful: Road work
Ralentir.................	Slow down
Rappel..................	Reminder (speed limit, to slow down in a town)
Bande d'urgence	Breakdown lane
Toutes directions	All directions
Centre ville	Center of town
Aire....................	Rest stop (with or without services)
Sortie...................	Exit
Péage...................	Toll (tollbooth sign)

Michelin maps are excellent. Regional road maps by the *Institut Géographique National* indicate tourist information. You can almost always get free maps of a town, just by stopping at the tourist office. Look for the words *Syndicat d'Initiative,* or a capital *I.*

Parking Spots

On-street parking is at a premium in cities. Large parking lots or underground parking garages are usually the solution. These will be indicated by blue signs with a capital *P.* The word is the same as in English, *parking,* though on-street parking might be called *stationnement.* If you see a sign that says *stationnement interdit* or *stationnement gênant,* do not park there.

In parking lots or spaces on the street, you'll often have to feed coins into a ticket machine, called a *horodateur,* which will provide a ticket to place on your dashboard. The *horodateur* will be marked, but you may have to look up and down the street or across the parking lot for a rectangular box with buttons and dials.

Information on the *horodateur* will indicate how much change you need to feed the machine for the time you'll be gone. Parking is usually free from noon to two o'clock, so don't include this period in your payment. For example, if you park at 11:00 a.m. and expect to be gone for shopping and lunch until 3 p.m., pay for two hours, not four.

Insert the required coins and the machine will indicate the end time. When you've reached the time required, push the green button. A ticket will slide out, indicating your parking deadline. Place this on the driver's side of the dashboard in a visible spot.

A Word to the Wise

When parking in France, avoid leaving belongings visible in your car. It's a temptation for thieves.

On the positive side, when you live in France and your car is licensed locally, it will be less of a target than one that's obviously a rental, which is read as a trunk-full of luggage.

In small towns off the tourist path, leaving small things in the car is not usually a big problem. In other areas, even leaving a water bottle is liable to result in a broken window.

Be especially careful in Paris, Provence, and any popular tourist area.

15
Allô, Allô? Is Anyone There?

"THE TIME HAS COME," THE WALRUS SAID,
"TO TALK OF MANY THINGS."
—Lewis Carroll, *Through the Looking-Glass*

Communications in France are modern and efficient, and they present you with a range of public and private phone services, plus computer and Internet options. France Télécom operates the phone system and sells the majority of phone products and services.

DIALING DIGITS

Phone numbers in France consist of eight digits that are written like a Noah's Ark of numbers, two by two. These are often shown with periods between each of the pairs of digits, such as 12.34.56.78.

The Disappearing "0"

When dialing a phone number within France, you must precede it with a zero and a digit 1 to 5, indicating a region of the country. Paris, for example, is in region 1 so you would dial a 01 plus the eight digits of the phone number. Regardless of where you're calling in France, dial the 0 plus the region code. Note that the 0 is dialed only *within* France. If you are dialing a French number from the United States or any other country, drop the 0. For such a call, dial the international operator, the country code (33) for France, the region number 1 to 5, then the eight-digit phone number.

Many guidebooks and brochures haven't caught up with the regional numbers yet, and may not provide the 0+(region number). Check the front of a phone book for a map that shows the regions and their numbers.

Colorful 800 Numbers

France has a series of 800-type numbers, not all of which are free. The "green numbers" or *Numero Vert* begin with 08 00. These numbers are free.

"Azure numbers" or *Numero Azur* begin with 08 01. These numbers discount the price of a long-distance call, providing it at the same tariff as a local call.

Numbers beginning with 08 such as 08 02 and 08 03 are not free or discounted. In fact, they cost more.

Phone Books

When we first moved here, I translated "phone book" into *livre de téléphone* and requested one at the phone company. All I got was a peculiar look from the clerk. The proper name for a phone book in France is an *annuaire*.

Ask for your first one when you sign up for phone service. In succeeding years, you'll receive a notice in the mail, indicating to go to the local post office to pick up the new one. *La Poste* also provides a bin to recycle the old phone books.

Using a Télécarte

A *Télécarte* is the handy electronic phone card that's required on virtually all French public phones. The cards provide prepaid units, which are valid for local or long-distance calls. The cards automatically count down the time remaining. *Télécartes* can be purchased at France Télécom offices, post offices, tobacco stores (*tabac*), and other stores that display the words "*Télécartes en vente ici.*" Cards can also be purchased via automatic distributors in train stations, airports, and large shopping centers. *Télécartes* cost 49 FF ($8.60) for 50 units and 97,50 FF ($17) for 120 units.

To use a public phone lift the handset (*décrochez*), insert the *Télécarte*, wait for the tone, then dial the phone number. The phone will display the number of units you have left on your card and count them down as you talk. When you hang up, remember to take your card back. It's amazing how many people forget.

If the number you're calling is busy, or there's no answer, the public phone will ask if you want to leave a message. If you do so, the automated system will recall the number up to four times to deliver the message.

Phone booths provide free calls to emergency numbers (15, 17, 18) and France Télécom services.

EMERGENCY NUMBERS

France's equivalent of 911 is really three different numbers:

18   Fire and Emergency   Sapeurs Pompiers*
17   Police/Ambulance   Gendarmerie Police
15   Medical Emergency   Soins Medicaux Urgents (SAMU)*

* For more explanation on how these function in medical emergencies, see chapter 21, "A Toast to Your Health."

YOUR PHONE AT HOME

Arranging phone service is as simple as visiting the nearest France Télécom office. The representative will suggest numerous levels of service, and will help you pick the most economical plan, based on your calling patterns.

Sign up for the detailed phone bill (*facturation détaillée*), which is free and provides valuable information on the time, date, duration, destination, and exact cost of each phone call.

Costs and Discounts

The monthly service fee each month is inexpensive, but each call, including locals ones, are metered. This adds up to a big change for Americans, who are accustomed to unlimited local calls.

The phone bill arrives every two months and includes the monthly phone charge (*abonnement*) two months in advance, plus the last two months of actual charges, rated according to local, neighboring, national, international, and special services.

The tariff depends on the distance of the call and the time you call. Local calls at full tariff are currently billed at .28/minute FF ($.05), or .14/minute FF ($.02) during off hours. As may be expected, the most expensive times to call are the prime business hours, 8 a.m. to 7 p.m. Monday through Friday. Evenings, weekends, and holidays are less costly calling times.

The basic monthly fee of 78 FF ($13) includes maintenance, line service, and the detailed bill. France Télécom offers a wide variety of special calling plans that provide discounts for local calls (*Forfait Local*), commonly dialed numbers (*Primalist*), and special options (*Primalist Pays* or *Primalist Internet*). Be sure to ask which plan will be best for you when you sign up for service.

Overseas Calls

To call the United States or any other country outside France, dial a code for the international operator (00) then the country code (1 for the U.S., for example), the city code, and the local number. You can do this from any phone. The trick is to find the most efficient and economical means of chatting with friends and family across an ocean.

Long-distance calls to the United States are 2 FF ($.33) per minute normal tariff or 1,60 FF ($.26) per minute reduced tariff. The reduced tariff to United States and Canada applies from seven in the evening to noon the next day during the week, plus weekends and holidays. Calls to Great Britain are 1,85 FF ($.31) a minute or 1,45 FF ($.24) a minute reduced tariff.

Home Phone Discounts

France Télécom offers discounts on various service plans as mentioned above. Two discounts are particularly helpful in dialing the States: *Primalist* and *Primalist Pays* services.

As a *Primalist* subscriber, you pay 10 FF (about $1.67) per month, which earns a discount of twenty-five percent on the six numbers called most often. These can be local or overseas calls. You don't even have to select the six numbers, the France Télécom computer does it automatically. The discount applies twenty-four hours a day, seven days a week. Note that, because it applies on local calls, your discount may not go to U.S. calls, if you call six friends around the corner more than you call your kids in California.

On *Primalist*, one minute to the States costs just 1,20 FF ($.20). At 20 cents a minute, these are currently among the lowest rates we've found. Costs are continually changing with competition, however, so compare. Also compare the monthly service fee. *Primalist* is only 10 FF ($1.67) for the discount; other services can charge up to $10 a month.

Primalist Pays is another excellent choice for an expatriate living in France. For 10 FF ($1.67) a month, you save twenty-five percent on your calls to one foreign country of your choice. The discount applies seven days a week, twenty-four hours a day. This discount applies even to the low, non-prime hour tariff. This plan is ideal for those who make a lot of calls to family, friends, or the person taking care of their cat in the U.S.

Call-back Providers

A call-back service provider has lines leased, which they use to provide access to less-expensive phone service. You dial the number they provide, then hang up. They call you back (hence the name), then you dial the number of the party you wish to call. Call-back rates usually apply twenty-four hours a day, so you can call when you want, not wait for special evening or holiday rates.

Call-back services advertise in the *New York Times* and *International Herald Tribune*. The largest of these call-back providers is Kallback, which bills U.S.-bound calls at 20 cents per minute, Canada calls at 33 cents per minute, and calls to the UK at 28 cents per minute. They sometimes tack on a $10 monthly fee, depending on which offer you respond to. I asked specifically and the representative said there wasn't a fee when I signed on, then I noticed later that it had been added to the bill. When I questioned them, they removed the charge.

Long-Distance Calling Cards

AT&T, Sprint, MCI, and others offer calling cards that provide access to English-speaking operators. The cards work on most public and private phones. To use a calling card, dial an access number for the country you're calling, the number you want, plus the calling card number, which serves as a security code.

If you already have an AT&T or another calling card, the card is probably tied to a home or office phone number. You'll be able to use the card only if you maintain that home or business number while you're in France. When you cancel that phone number, the card is no longer valid. To avoid this problem, request a "direct billed" card, which is not tied to a home phone number but is billed to a major credit card, such as American Express, VISA, or MasterCard.

Since they provide the extra services of English-speaking operators, these U.S. calling card calls are much more expensive than automated call-back providers or even your home phone in France. I'd recommend using them only when you're dialing from a hotel that might otherwise tack on excessive fees or when you are desperate.

Another service offered by AT&T is USA Direct, which connects you with an AT&T operator who speaks English. You can use it to call any location in the States, except Alaska, from more than 120 countries and locations around the world; however, you pay dearly for the operator service.

AT&T's World Connect service works like USA Direct, but it functions from one foreign country to another foreign country. If you're in France, for example, and are planning to go to Switzerland, you can call for hotel reservations using World Connect. To use USA Direct or World Connect, you'll pay a fee of $2.50 per connection, plus you pay for the first minute at a certain rate and are metered for each additional minute. The card can also be used within the United States for an 80-cent-per-minute surcharge. With prices like this, this card is only for dire emergencies or businessmen on expense accounts.

Internet

Major Internet service providers provide local numbers or a number that, even if long distance, is metered at local rates. This is a shock to Americans, however, since Internet access can be quite expensive if you're a real cyber-nut.

For a fifty percent discount, subscribe to France Télécom's service, *Primalist Internet,* for 10 FF (about $1.67) a month. The discount applies when you connect to your Internet service provider between 10 p.m. to 8 a.m. the next morning.

LE BON MOT: PHONE SERVICE

Abonné	Subscriber
Abonnement	Subscription to phone service
Annuaire	Telephone directory
Compte	Account
Date Facture	Billing date
Facture	Bill
Facture détaillée	Detailed bill
H.T. (hors taxe)	Excluding TVA
Pages jaunes	Yellow pages
Total de la TVA	Including TVA
Solde	Balance left on account

France Télécom

France Télécom sells a wide range of telephones, including portable phones (*le téléphone sans-fil*) which are highly popular in France. They also sell fax machines (*le fax*), answering machines (*le répondeur*), Minitel (see page 122), and accessories for phone products.

Handy France Télécom Services

Optional phone services include call transfer (*transfert d'appel*), which lets you forward a call to another number, call waiting (*signal d'appel*), which notifies you of an incoming call and allows you to put the first caller on hold, and conference calls (*conversation à trois*).

Our favorite, since we never seem to have a working alarm clock, is the reminder service (*memo d'appel*). You can use this anytime. Just dial *55* then the time you want to be called. Use the 24-hour clock. For example, 6:30 in the morning would be 0630; 6:30 at night would be 1830. Finish with the pound sign. Thus, that wake-up call would be *55*0630# for the morning call; *55*1830# for the evening call. The charge is 3,71 FF ($.62) for each *memo d'appel*, billed to your phone bill.

Your phone bill can be handled with a *prélevement* just as your other utilities. Remember to request an itemized bill (*une facture détaillée*). There's no extra charge for it, and otherwise you'll just receive the total amount.

Mobile Phones

Portable phones are ubiquitous in France. It's quite a contrast to see people talking and strolling on Paris streets or in small villages, past centuries-old walls. Mobile phone service uses the Global System for Mobile Communication, which works only in France and most other European countries, so don't plan to bring your cell phone from the States.

LE BON MOT: PHONE CALLS

Allô	Hello (on the phone)
Annuaire	Telephone directory
Appel	Telephone call
Composez le numero	Dial the number
Coup de fil	Phone call (idiomatic)
Décrochez	Answer the phone
Ne quittez pas	Don't hang up
Qui est à l'appareil?	Who's speaking?
Raccrochez	Hang up
Tonalité	Dial tone

Minitel

The world's first populist computer system began in France and is called the Minitel. Don't expect the glorious graphics of the Internet, but the Minitel provides text services to every phone subscriber who wants the opportunity to check phone numbers, weather, stocks, travel services, news, restaurant bookings, computer dating, ticketing, and much more. You'll see these in post offices, where you can ask to use them. The clerk will help you learn, but reserve this request for a slow time.

To do a Minitel search, turn on the unit, dial a code number on your telephone, wait for the tone, then type in the code and press *Connexion Fin.* When you're finished, press *Connexion Fin* again to quit the connection— and avoid a massive bill. Information remains on the screen until the terminal's switched off, so you can study that train schedule without paying more.

Minitel terminals range from simple base units to advanced systems with all the bells and whistles. A France Télécom representative can explain the differences. You buy the terminal and pay for services as you use them.

Connection fees are charged by the minute. The first few minutes are free for directory services, then there is a charge for specialized services, usually about 2 FF ($ .33) per minute, though it varies. The exact charges for the service you're requesting are listed when you first make the connection.

A recent addition to the Minitel is free e-mail access, so if you otherwise have no use for a computer, this would be a less expensive option for staying in touch with family and friends via e-mail.

U.S. 800 Numbers
When you dial U.S. 800 numbers from France, they are not toll-free, since you'll have to pay to reach the U.S. phone system. Whether you're using a private phone, a call-back service, or a calling card, you'll pay normal long-distance rates.

Computers
My computer is arranged so that I have a view of our garden and the grapevine that sprawls across the rear of our house. This distracts me from working, but it can also help. The *ordinateur* (computer) can keep you from the marvels in France, if you spend hours on-line instead of exploring. It's certainly not a necessity in France.

That said, I'm a fervent fan of the computer. If you want to keep in close touch with family, friends, and others, or take advantage of the marvelous travel, news, and educational services available, a computer is a fine thing to have handy.

You can purchase computer equipment in France. It will have French software and a French keyboard, however, which will add to your difficulties.

The simpler solution is to bring a computer with you from the United States. A notebook size is handy and easy to transport. It offers the additional benefit of including an adaptable power supply, which enables it to be used in France without a transformer. You just need the plug adapter to fit the different shape of the French electric socket. A further advantage of the notebook-size computer is the ability to take it on travels through Europe, should you want to keep in touch on a long vacation.

A desktop computer can be used with a transformer to convert the power supply. Or, order your computer built with an adaptable power supply when you purchase the computer.

Another solution is to purchase your computer in England or Ireland. You can buy the computer (great excuse for a visit) and bring it back yourself. Even easier, make a phone call and order from one of the international suppliers, such as Gateway or Dell, who will ship computer products directly to your door in France. If you order from one of these companies, be sure to explain that you want English language software and keyboards but French current, plugs, and modem.

Internet Service Providers
France offers numerous Internet service providers, or ISPs. Among them are France Télécom's Wanadoo service and AOL, which is the largest Internet provider that crosses European borders. ISPs in France charge approxi-

mately the same as services do in the States. As I mentioned, in Europe the phone connection is metered per minute, adding to the costs of staying on-line.

Free Internet services are starting to appear. FNAC, a French chain store specializing in electronics and books, now offers no-charge Internet connection. Others are following. AOL began offering free Internet service in Britain and may extend it to France and the continent later. As competition heats up, things will change rapidly, so check for the best deal when you arrive.

One of the nicest things about France is the absence of spam mail, those advertising e-mails that crowd out your important messages and waste on-line time. This is strictly controlled on French Internet services.

You'll find cyber-cafés in large cities, enabling you to go on-line for an hourly charge, to check your e-mail or search the Internet wherever you travel in France. Recently, some post offices have added computers and offer a "smart card" that enables you to log on in any participating *Poste.*

Le Bon Mot: Computer-ese

Abonnement	Internet service subscription
Cartouche	Printer cartridge
Clavier	Keyboard
Écran	Screen
E-mail	E-mail
Imprimante	Printer
Mot de passe	Password
Ordinateur	Computer
Software	Software
Souris	Mouse

Postal Services

Royal blue and bright yellow jackets are a common sight in France, as mailmen and women make their rounds, delivering mail via car, foot, bicycle, and motor scooters.

The mail system is highly efficient and the most amazing thing is that letters sent within France arrive anywhere else in the country the very next day. (If you say, "The check's in the mail," it had better be!)

Sending mail to areas outside of France is another story entirely. You can count on a letter reaching the United States in anywhere from four to five days. Packages take longer, unless you pay special delivery charges or send them Fed Ex, UPS, or Airborne.

Incoming mail from the States takes the same amount of time and usually arrives as expected, except for a few horror stories. One package from a friend arrived in such shreds that the only thing holding the two brochures inside together was an inch of shredded brown paper. Another package filled with our forwarded mail was sent right after we moved here, and has never shown up. Ever since, we've had important mail sent via a traceable service. It costs more, but after dealing with the hassles (and the rumor that a check was in the shipment that we'll never ever see), we're adding the special shipping charges to the price of living in our paradise.

La Poste

A post office (*la Poste*) is found in virtually every town in France, and provides stamps, handy preposted envelopes, and other services. The post office also provides a Minitel for customer use, and sometimes has pay phones available with people to help you figure out the calling system. *La Poste* is even the bank for thousands of people. (For more on the financial services offered by *la Poste*, see chapter 16, page 132)

Post office hours vary, depending on the location. In major cities the main post offices will be open all day, from approximately 9:00 a.m. to 7:00 p.m. In small towns, the post office, like most businesses, will close for lunch hour(s). Days of the week will usually be Monday through Friday, with a half-day on Saturday, though in small villages, hours will depend on the whim of the clerk.

The post office distributes phone books when they come out each year, usually in March. If you have a phone, you'll receive a notice in the mail, which you turn in for your *annuaire*.

Fees

Postage costs 3 FF ($.50) for a letter delivered within the country. To the United States, a normal letter will cost 4,40 FF ($.73).

PostExport and Chronopost are preposted cardboard envelopes that have postage to various part of the world. Look for the ones for *États-Unis*. The PostExports are especially handy, as they come in two sizes. The small envelope will take 100 grams of weight for 15 FF ($2.50), or a handy 500-gram size that holds typewritten pages unfolded costs 50 FF ($8.33). PostExport is delivered to the States within four to six days.

If you want something faster, Chronopost is the express-mail service; it takes one to two days, which depends, according to the *Poste* disclaimer, on whether or not the destination is a major city (*grande ville*) and whether the package will have to make numerous stops along the way.

La *Poste* sells packs of preposted note cards and greeting cards, which change in design periodically based on current events or trends. They include a handy five-pack of envelopes with matching notes for 30 FF ($5). The greeting cards are high quality and feature light-hearted designs. At 14 FF ($2.33), they're an excellent value compared to those found in most stationery stores—and the price includes postage. After much review of every card rack in the immediate 100 miles, whose birthday cards feature pallid forget-me-nots for 16 FF ($2.50) or more, *la Poste* is now my first stop when sending birthday wishes.

Le Bon Mot: Decoding Postal Lingo

Affranchir	To apply postage
Boîte à lettres	Post box
Code postal	Zip code
Colis	Package
Courrier	Mail
Destinataire	Person letter/package is directed to
Expéditeur	Person sending the letter/package
Facteur	Mailman/woman
Lettre	Letter
Paquet	Package
Par avion	Airmail
Poste	Post office
Pré-timbré	Prestamped
Timbre	Stamp

Lifestyles: Writing Life in the Dordogne

When John and Betsy Braden moved to Le Soulier in southwest France, the number of residents in their hamlet rose to 32. Being a rare species of *humanis americanis*, they put French lessons high on the agenda.

Does this intimidate them? No way. The move to France was an opportunity for the writer/photographer team to practice what they preached, with a long-term stay in France. "Given our vagabond bent, we feel at home in Europe. We were ready to decamp."

Why a small village, far from the bright lights? "We discovered the area because a French friend lived nearby and fell in love with the area," says Betsy.

Their rental cottage is tucked into a rocky cliff, on a steep road that winds upwards to provide, at the top, a magnificent view of a lake far below. Surrounding them are hills as powerfully green as AstroTurf, rugged rock faces, gorges, thermal spas, prehistoric caves, and castles tucked high on cliff faces. Days fly by with visits to nearby Brive-la-Gaillarde, a town of 3,500, where they explore narrow passageways and small shops that offer the regional specialties of *foie gras* and truffles. A half-hour west is Perigueux, a city presenting greater choices. A quiet trip to the nearby vineyards of Medoc (Mouton-Rothschild and St.-Emilion) ensures a stock of good wine for meals on the terrace.

When they're feeling creative, the couple spends time with travel writing and photography assignments, something they're eager to do more of for the happy reason that "the more potluck assignments we find, the longer we can stay here!"

16
Money Whispers

IT IS EASY TO GET EVERYTHING YOU WANT, PROVIDED YOU FIRST
LEARN TO DO WITHOUT THE THINGS YOU CANNOT GET.
—Elbert Hubbard

Though no one in France would turn down *le Loto* if they won it, the topic of money is greatly frowned upon as a topic of conversation. This is a shocking change for an American, who considers "What do you do for a living?" to be normal cocktail-party banter. Not in France, where this conversation-starter is equivalent to asking how much someone makes, as though you're trying to decide if they're worth talking to.

In normal business dealings, any owed money is handled discretely. I wish I had a franc for every time I've asked a service person how much I owed for a product or service, only to be put off with small talk or told that they'd send the bill later. It's enough to make you feel like a heathen, having mentioned such a crass subject.

Of course, in some parts of the country, notably Paris, the French are becoming almost as money-grubbing as Americans, but in the countryside, the traditional attitude prevails: Money is not a genteel topic of conversation.

CURRENCY: FRANC AND EURO

Even the French can't avoid discussing the conversion of the franc to the euro. France will share this new currency with ten other European nations that are currently in the process of adopting it. The euro will be used by all these countries as the common currency. This will make crossing borders (and European vacations from your French home) easier, by eliminating a stop for currency exchange. It will also enable consumers to make comparisons more easily between the apple-red French sweater and the orange Italian one, without exchange rates confusing the issue.

While this transition from the franc to the euro is happening, you'll be dealing with the franc, which is used for everyday transactions at the bakery and butcher, but the price in euros is already being shown alongside that of the franc in stores, on bank-account statements, and in other financial dealings.

The euro currency will be put into circulation on 1 January 2002, and both that and the French currency will be used temporarily. On 1 July 2002, the franc will disappear completely.

The French Franc

Until the euro becomes a physical entity, the French franc remains the currency of France. It's available in bills of 20, 50, 100, 200, and 500. Just to make things confusing, francs come in the form of coins as well as bills. There are 1-, 2-, 5-, 10-, and 20-franc coins. Thus, you can have a 20-franc coin or a 20-franc note. They're worth the same thing.

There are 100 centimes in a franc and centimes are available as 5-, 10-, 20-, and 50-centime coins.

Exchange Rates

The dollar-to-franc and dollar-to-euro exchange rate varies, of course. However, the euro-to-franc exchange rate has been set in stone at 1 euro equals 6,55957 francs. (Note that the comma in France is like the American decimal point, which makes it approximately 6.6 in English. See below for more explanation.)

An easy trick to convert from francs to euros is to add the amount in francs to half its value, then divide by 10. Thus, an item at 250 francs would be equal to 250 plus 125, which is 375, divided by 10, which equals 37.50.

It's a lot easier to downsize here, because people aren't as materialistic.
You can have friends from all walks of life, and they don't care
how much money you make.
—Sara, the Ardèche

What's That Number?

When dealing with bills and banking, you'll want to get your numbers right. Most people know that Europeans like to put a little line through the seven so that it looks like this: 7. But that doesn't prepare you for a one, which always looks like a seven to Americans. And fours look like nines. Here's what you're likely to see.

1 2 3 4 5 6 7 8 9

The French franc is written as FF or simply F. Also confusing is that where Americans use a period, the French use a comma, and vice versa. Five francs and twenty-five centimes is written 5,25 FF. Five thousand francs and twenty-five centimes is written 5.000,25 FF.

Cost of Living

France is not an inexpensive country, though it's possible to live well here without being Bill Gates.

The most shocking expenses are energy-related. Gasoline to fill your car's tank costs the equivalent of about $4.50 a gallon. This is one reason that public transportation and private feet (as in walking and biking) are a lot more popular in France than in the States.

Electricity is also expensive, although France's nuclear power plants produce electricity in such abundant quantity that they're able to export it to other European countries, such as Germany. The thrifty French simply insulate their homes, monitor their appliance use, and don't heat rooms they don't use.

Food, of course, is one of the joys of living in France. This is one area where costs are not exorbitant. Local produce enables you to eat like a *roi*, enjoying the flavor inherent in the freshest of fresh foods. However, if you insist on imported products, you'll pay dearly for the joy of having that jar of taco sauce.

Restaurant meals depend on your budget and gourmet tastes, but you can enjoy a four-course lunch with wine in a small *café* off the tourist route for 70 francs ($12) or less. Naturally, you can pay ten times that in a Michelin-rated establishment, with five waiters hovering over your caviar and truffle soup.

Many couples in France share one car, because public transportation is so good. In Paris, you don't need a car at all. So put that money into the apartment costs, which will be higher than in the French countryside.

Other things that are more costly than in the States are clothing and paper products, such as greeting cards, laser paper for your printer, and English-language books imported from the United States.

Socially, there's a lot less pressure to have money here.
You can drive a Clio here and not feel self-conscious.

—Cary, Pau

BANK SERVICES

You'll be held up at the entrance of every French bank. This is not a comment on rampant crime, but on the fact that bank security systems keep the bad guys at bay (and the good customers waiting) in a small anteroom inside an outer door. Ring a bell, and the teller will push a button to release the latch that lets you in the lobby. Once inside, the tellers are at desks or a counter, with no bulletproof glass between you and them. In short, nothing except faulty French will prevent an exchange of financial facts.

Banks in France include commercial banks and savings banks that are cooperatives. Commercial banks include *Crédit Lyonnais, Banque National de Paris* (BNP), and *Societé Générale.* Cooperative banks are *Crédit Agricole, Crédit Mutuel,* and *Banque Populaire.* Most of these banks have branches throughout France in cities. Even small towns are served by one or more of the cooperative banks.

La Poste

The post office offers a range of banking services, including checking and savings accounts and loans. Many people use the post office to arrange money transfers, bill payment, and debit cards. A big advantage of *la Poste* is the fact that post offices are located throughout France, even in the smallest villages. You'll always be near one, and the opening hours are usually longer than at banks, too.

Post offices are now adding automated teller machines (ATMs) outside their entrances. These ATMs accept the major bank debit cards, such as Cirrus, so even if you don't have a postal bank account, you can withdraw money.

It was a major event in our town when our post office added that little gizmo—and it is very convenient to my house.

Checking Accounts

You can easily open a checking account in France by following the same basic procedures you would in the United States. If you want to open an account before you make the move, to pay security deposits or otherwise set up your household, visit the bank when making a preliminary visit.

Or, you can open an account without even setting foot in France. One bank, *Banque Transatlantique,* is specially designed to serve expatriates. Financial services include checking accounts (in any currency), advice on asset management, international taxation, and more. Since services are offered in English, it's like having a French checking account with training wheels. Their U.S. address is 1819 J St. NW, Suite 620, Washington DC 20006; telephone: (202) 429 1909; website: *http://www.transat.tm.fr.* *Banque Transatlantique*'s main office is in Paris, but it's part of the *CIC Banques* group, so you can transfer your account to a local branch elsewhere in the country.

Savings banks in France, such as *Caisses d'Epargne,* offer some services, though fewer than the other banks. These are member-only banks and do not provide services for nonmembers, so don't try changing money here.

Our account at Banque Transatlantique came in handy for more than just checking....
We were stranded a day in Paris, lugging around heavy bags, because the lockers
had been closed at the train stations. We didn't know what to do,
but they talk about personal service, so we went to the bank. They kept
our luggage so we could wander around unencumbered!
—John, Loire Valley

Credit Cards

For a socialist country, the French have taken to capitalism in a big way. Once ensconced in the system, you'll have opportunities to take loans and be in debt, just like in America. When our ten-year-old Citroën was ready for life-support, the bill was temporarily beyond our means. No problem. We were promptly provided with a handy-dandy American Express/Citroën card, which provides charge privileges, gives us discounts based on a point system for the amount charged, and offers a special long-term no-interest system for Citroën services. The car got a new life and we got six months to pay for the repairs.

We occasionally receive offers through these charge cards to give us 2000 or 5000 francs, just for the fun of it. As in the States, interest accrues. We've wisely turned these "generous offers" down.

Carte Bleue

Carte Bleue is the most commonly held debit card in France and is accepted in large supermarkets, stores, and restaurants throughout the country. You must know your four-digit PIN, which the bank provides with the card, because you'll be asked to punch it in as an approval. (Don't keep it on the card!)

Because *Carte Bleue* is a debit card, not a credit card, be sure to jot down the amount of your purchase and deduct it immediately from your checking account before you forget and overdraw your account, which is even more of a no-no in France than in the U.S.

Prélevements

Most regular bills in France—utilities, telephone, mortgage, and such—are handled via automatic deduction from your checking account, called *prélevement.* When you first establish your billing account, you will be asked to supply a *TIP,* which stands for *Titre Interbancaire de Paiement.* You will find several of these forms behind the checks in your checkbook. If you need extras, just request them at your bank and show your checkbook.

You'll receive a statement for the amount to be billed, with the date the money will be withdrawn from your checking account. Write down this date immediately, because it will be easy to forget. Then deduct the amount from your checkbook on the proper date each billing period.

If you're forgetful like me, you should periodically check the previous month's statement and note which bills are deducted when. Write this information into the ledger for the coming month, to ensure you keep enough money in your checking account.

Some companies do not send monthly bills to remind you of a *préleve-ment.* Instead you may get a statement telling you the company will deduct each payment monthly for the entire year. It's up to you to keep track and deduct money on schedule.

The system makes bill-paying easier, with no checks to write or envelopes to post. If you want to travel, you're free to come and go as you please. The bills will be deducted whether you're at home or not. We thought our phone bill was being deducted when we made one two-month trip back to the States, but returned to discover I hadn't filled out the TIP properly. We were being threatened with losing the phone service, though they never cut the cord. I quickly sent in the proper paperwork and now we're free to roam again.

Overdrawing is more problematic in France than in the United States. It can blacken your credit and may result in the bank closing your checking account. Learn to balance your checking account accurately and ask about insurance on the account, which will cover minor mistakes and possibly losses if your bank card is lost or stolen.

U.S.-Based Income

Most Americans living in France maintain bank accounts and investments in the United States. Depending on your situation, a checking account usually comes in handy, to pay U.S. bills or to serve as a repository for U.S. income, whether it's salary, pension, or Social Security.

Concerning Social Security, Americans who retire in France can apply for and receive Social Security in France by contacting the U.S. embassy in Paris. Apply several months prior to the date you want to begin to receive the payments, since it takes a bit longer to process the paperwork from France.

In France, all Social Security and other federal payments, such as veteran's benefits, must be paid into bank accounts electronically. Tax refunds are also available for expatriates electronically. Having the payments automatically deposited into your U.S. checking account works very well because you can draw the money as you need it via an automatic teller machine in France. You'll receive your francs at an excellent rate of exchange.

U.S. Taxes

If you have any income in the United States, whether from a salary or investments, you are obligated to file a U.S. (and possibly state) tax return. If you are overseas on April 15 and expect to owe tax, you can make payments with Extension Forms 2350 or 4868, to avoid interest charges. The Overseas Filer due date is June 15.

Income-tax returns cannot be filed with the IRS in Paris. They should be mailed directly to the IRS in the United States: Internal Revenue Service, Philadelphia, PA 19255-0207.

Estimated tax payments, with the Form 1040-ES payment voucher, should be mailed directly to the Internal Revenue Service, PO Box 8318, Philadelphia, PA 19255.

Payments must be made by check in U.S. dollars, made payable to the Internal Revenue Service. For more information, contact the Internal Revenue Service before you leave the States or contact the IRS at the American embassy in Paris. Taxpayer assistance is provided on a first-come, first-served basis. They will not, in any case, prepare your returns unless you are elderly and handicapped. However, there are tax experts in Paris who specialize in tax returns for American expatriates. Request recommendations from the embassy or other Americans in France.

The IRS office is located in the U.S. Consulate, 2, rue St. Florentin, Paris; *Métro*: Concorde. The mailing address is the American embassy around the corner at 2, avenue Gabriel, 75382 Paris, Cedex 08. For short questions, call the IRS at 01 43 12 25 55. For longer questions or technical information, send a written query or fax to 01 43 12 47 52.

You can also find IRS information in France through websites: *http://www.amb-usa.fr* or *http://www.irs.ustreas.gov*. If you have a Minitel in France, you can get other tax information by dialing 3614 Etats-Unis.

Le Bon Mot: Talking Money

Argent	Money (in general)
Billet	Note
Bourse	Stock exchange
Bureau de change	Foreign exchange
Cheque	Check
Cheque de banque	Bank draft
Chequier	Checkbook
Compte	Account
Créditer	To credit the account
Débiter	To debit the account
Dépot	Deposit
Distributeur	Automated teller machine (ATM)
Espèces	Cash
Monnaie	Change
Prélevement	Automatic deduction
Relevé	Statement
Retrait	Withdrawal
Versement	Payment
Virement	Bank transfer

17
At Your Leisure

THE QUALITY OF A LIFE IS DETERMINED BY ITS ACTIVITIES.
—Aristotle

"Aren't you bored?"

That question slipped from the lips of off-season visitors who repeated it three times, when they noticed that our small town shutters itself into suspended animation every evening and all day Tuesday. They'd just arrived from the bright lights of Paris, just fifty minutes away by fast train.

How does one answer such a question? First, some people prefer the big-city life. That's why many Americans choose to live in Paris. I love the city too and succumb to its thrills on a regular basis. That doesn't mean everyone must live there.

One of the chief pleasures of France is the tranquillity found in the countryside. Tranquillity is not a synonym for boredom.

Every area of France, city or country, offers a wealth of historic and artistic sights to be explored, from World War II beaches to prehistoric cave paintings, from Roman amphitheaters to *châteaux*, cathedrals, and museums, each with its unique history and art.

Even without those special activities, daily life in France is a fascinating kaleidoscope. The markets, for example, entice you to spend extra hours for simple shopping, encouraging an in-depth study of the current season's produce—with appropriate comments and comparisons—before deciding on the ingredients for the night's dinner.

Time and again, fresh discoveries present themselves, as you peel down the layers and dig deeper into your area of France. That simple church in an out-of-the-way village may be built over a crypt decorated with eleventh-century frescoes, or a little-known chateau may have the letter Marie Antoinette wrote to her children in the dawn hours before she was guillotined.

Exploration and enjoyment are reasons you've chosen to live in France so make the most of it. Remember the French phrase: *On doit profiter.* Or, enjoy the moment. There are hundreds of ways to do just that.

THE ARTS

France does not put art on a pedestal; it showcases it in every park and thoroughfare, including the Paris *Métro*, with its musicians, who are licensed to entertain there. Art in France is an active part of everyday life, not an occasional pastime. It's this daily enjoyment and acceptance of art that has enthralled so many painters, writers, sculptors, and musicians, encouraging them to settle here.

Real Steals

For those in the know, special offers cut your cost of viewing exceptional French art. One pass, in particular, benefits the person who stays in France longer than a two-week vacation. The National Monuments Pass (*Laissez Passes de la Caisse Nationale des Monuments Historique et des Sites*) provides unlimited free entrance to participating national monuments for a year from the date of purchase. It includes more than 100 sites, 16 of which are located in the area near Paris; the rest of the sites are located throughout France. Check the available brochure before you purchase the pass, however, to see if the sites you want to see are included, as the sites are scattered and are not necessarily major ones. The pass costs 280 FF (about $47). You can find the National Monuments Pass at participating monuments or at the *Caisse Nationale des Monuments Historique et des Sites*; telephone: 01 44 61 21 50.

The Paris Museum Pass (*La Carte des Musées et Monuments*) is the best deal if you want a quick hit of art and culture in a few days. It provides access to many of the most popular museums and monuments without waiting in line. (If you've ever seen the line snaking around the Louvre's pyramid, you know why this is a good idea.) The pass enables you to unlimited visits to the permanent collections (not guided visits or temporary exhibitions) of seventy museums and monuments in Paris and the surrounding Île-de-France, during the days for which you've purchased the pass. Ask for the pass at participating museums and monuments, main

Métro stations, or the tourist offices at the Louvre Carrousel, Paris Tourist Office, or FNAC stores. The cost of the *Carte* depends on the number of days of use. A pass valid for one day costs 80 FF ($13), one for three days costs 160 FF ($27), and one for five days costs 240 FF ($40).

Regional passes are sometimes available for monuments in specific areas, such as the Loire or Provence-Alpes-Côte d'Azur. Check with the FNAC store or the *Caisse Nationale des Monuments Historiques et des Sites*, Hôtel de Sully, 62, rue Sainte-Antoine 75186 Paris, Cedex 04; telephone: 01 44 61 21 50.

Most museums offer discounts for children or seniors over sixty or sixty-five. Teachers and students usually get discount rates as well, so carry identification that proves your status. Sundays are good days for museum visits, as some museums are free or half price then.

A Few Reminders

Before setting out for a museum, check the hours. Some small museums close during the lunch hour, though they'll allow you to return afterwards—so keep your entry stub.

Most museums close one day a week, often Monday or Tuesday. Nothing's more disappointing than finding out that the museum you'd planned to visit that day is closed. Check the listings and schedule your visits accordingly. Many museums are closed on public holidays, and smaller ones may even close during *les vacances*, the month of August. Again, check the specific listing to save yourself disappointment and a wasted trip.

Sports

France provides ready access to virtually any sport you want to participate in, though you'd be hard-pressed to find a baseball or American-style football game. However, there are enough other sports to enjoy as a participant or armchair athlete. For the latter, you can sign up for EuroSport, the European ESPN—and the commentary's in English.

For information on sports activities in Paris, contact Allo-Sports at 01 42 76 54 54.

Here's a quick rundown of the most popular sports in France.

Soccer

Start learning to call soccer *football,* because you'll hear it often here in France, where *le foot* is the most popular sport. Adult's and children's teams are found throughout the country, and professional teams are followed closely.

When France played in the World Cup in France in 1998, the otherwise staid French citizens packed the streets, beeping horns, yelling "*Allez bleu*" for hours before the game; then the streets were silent, as *tout le monde* crowded into bars and sports halls to watch the match *en masse*.

For an idea of the atmosphere after France won, imagine the Super Bowl, World Series, and Fourth of July fireworks all rolled into one night.

Swimming

Pools, both outdoor and indoor, are common in cities and even small towns. Hours are usually designated for general use, families, or special events, such as swim meets. Beaches are, to the French, as honey is to a bear, and in August, when Europeans take *les vacances*, the world competes for their square meter of space. The crowds don't seem to bother the French, who consider the crowded beaches more convivial.

Tennis

Most French towns of any size also have public tennis courts and often tennis clubs. In Paris and large cities you'll find professional-level courts, but in the countryside, courts are made of easy-care painted concrete. If the weather's intemperate, you can play indoors in space shared with the basketball court—the floor is wood and has two sets of markings. I've often played a match, trying to distinguish the basketball lines from the tennis court.

The most famous French tennis tournament is the French Tennis Open, played at Roland Garros, 2, avenue Gordon Bennett, 75116 Paris; *Métro*: Porte d'Auteuil; telephone: 01 47 43 48 00; fax: 01 47 43 04 94. If you want to see this tournament in person, order tickets early via Minitel. Scalpers are out in force during the event, but there is no guarantee as to their tickets' legitimacy.

Skiing

What more could a skier want than the Alps at your backdoor? Downhill and cross-country (*ski au fond*) are both wildly popular in France, where most people take a winter break, often in February when the kids are on a midwinter holiday. Of course, you've got your choice of fabulous ski areas in France, but you're also within range of major ski areas of Switzerland, Austria, and Italy.

For information on winter sport locations, contact the tourist bureaus in the ski towns or the *Association des Maires des Stations Françaises de Sports d'Hiver*, 61, boulevard Haussmann, 75008 Paris; telephone: 01 47 42 23 32.

Horseback Riding

Stables offer lessons and riding opportunities in most areas of the country. One major area for the horse set is Saumur on the Loire River, which is home to the national riding school. Even nonriders can enjoy the special demonstrations held periodically. Summer is packed with horseback riding special events.

The Loire Valley, especially, has many stables and is popular for hunts. See your local tourist office for lists of stables that offer lessons or trail rides.

Golf
Golf courses are available in France, though they are neither as numerous nor as elaborate as in the United States. Prices are comparable to the States, ranging from the expensive private club memberships to casual nine-hole courses where you can play for a reasonable day rate.

Water Sports
Living on the coast, particularly the Mediterranean, is a sea-lover's paradise. Inland, lakes and rivers provide access to canoeing, kayaking, power boating, and sailing.

Fishing is popular on the seacoast, the lakes, and the many rivers that trace their way through France. A fishing license is necessary; check for signs posting the season.

Hunting
Hunting is popular for deer and small game. Areas of Sologne, the Loire, and the Berry make a spectator sport of hunts, where riding to the hounds is not just a sport of royal England. You'll find cars littering the sides of forested routes, while spectators watch for the dogs, who at any one time are liable to spill out onto the road, followed by the herd of red-jacketed, black-capped riders with bugles glinting in the sun.

Biking
France offers splendid opportunities for biking, either for pleasure or for the purpose of buying that morning's baguette. You can rent bikes, join a bike tour, or take your own bike with you on the train free of charge on most SNCF trains, including the TGV, though you must leave the bike in the baggage racks at the end of the cars. Some trains require that you bag the bike with the front wheel removed. Paris RER trains will accept bikes only during nonrush hours. The Paris *Métro* will not accept bikes at all.

You can also rent a bike at some SNCF stations. Call SNCF for more information at 01 53 90 20 20, or ask at your local station for a copy of the SCNF *Guide du Train et du Vélo*.

Bike riders are required to follow the rules of the road, which include riding on the right side of the road and not on the sidewalk (unless you're a child under eight). Obey red lights and signs for one-way streets.

Your bike must have front and rear lights, along with reflectors. And be sure to have a good lock that holds the frame and front tire.

The world's premier bike race, the Tour de France, lasts twenty-two days and is a grueling course. It's held every year in July and attempts to cover most areas of France. If your area is in the plans, local organizers note the route and list the start and finish areas, so you and your neighbors can get a curbside view.

Car Races
The famous Le Mans race raises the decibel level for miles around when it takes place for twenty-four hours in June. The cars wend past the town of Le Mans, which just happens to have a beautiful old town and cathedral. See it before you run out of gas.

Hiking/Walking
The fields, forests, and river paths of France provide ideal walking trails. Mind your walks, however, during hunting season, when the French hunters start off the day with a bit of a nip, then take off for woods or field.

A popular activity these days is the group walk, called a *randonnée*. These are discussed in more detail on page 50.

I do a lot of hiking, skiing, biking, canoeing, rafting....
I do it all, except mountain climbing. Where we live is sportsman's paradise
for water sports. We're just over an hour from Biarritz, which is
world-class surfing. Even the Hawaiians come there.
—Cary, Pau

LE BON MOT: SPORTING TERMS

Chasse . . . . Hunting
Le foot (football) . . . . Soccer
Piscine . . . . Swimming pool
Plage . . . . Beach
Randonnée . . . . Group walk, hike, or bike ride
Tennis . . . . Tennis
Vélo . . . . Bike

READING MATERIAL

Right after we moved to France, I had a sudden urge on a Friday night to hit a bookstore for a good mystery and cappuccino. Then I remembered that I was now living in a country where most people have never heard of Barnes & Noble or a hit of Starbuck's coffee.

If you love to read, as I do, you'll feel lost in France at first without easy access to English-language newspapers, magazines, and books. Don't fear, once you're in France, you'll find them and soon have stacks of reading material. But when you find them you'll have to first get over sticker shock. Reading material in France costs more than in the States, especially the imported English-language magazines and books.

Here's how you can get your reading materials and hopefully have enough left over for the coffee and croissant to enjoy with them.

Newspapers

USA Today, the *International Herald Tribune*, the *Wall Street Journal Europe*, and British papers, such as *The Financial Times* and the *Daily Telegraph*, can be found at news agents (*Maison de la Press*) and tobacco stores (*tabac*) throughout Paris and most good-size towns—even smaller towns, if they're in the tourist's path.

The *International Herald Tribune* publishes Monday through Saturday (except holidays) and provides same-day delivery of the newspaper right to your door via the French postal service. The system works fairly well, meaning that, if you're in Paris, you can count on delivery. Outside Paris, you will likely get the paper as expected, though occasionally it won't make the postman and you'll get it the next day. If you complain about late papers, the *IHT* will sometimes add a complimentary paper to your subscription. Notify the *IHT* when you're planning to be away from home, and they'll cease delivery until your return, extending the subscription to cover the number of papers you missed.

Magazines

English-language magazines can be found at English bookstores (see below). Free magazines in English include the *France-USA Contacts, Paris Free Voice*, and *Paris City Magazine*, all of which provide classifieds and entertainment news.

Practice French by perusing the countless glossy and picture-filled French magazines on every conceivable subject, from current events magazines such as the famous *Paris Match* to publications covering fashion, home, computers, and travel. Travel seems to be especially popular in France, with specialty magazines covering any region you might wish to visit.

Some U.S. magazines, such as *Time*, have international editions, which differ from the U.S. version but basically cover the same format. Some U.S. magazines will send your U.S. subscription to France, but they'll charge you a higher fee, due to the international postage. You'll have to decide if it's worth it to you.

You can buy U.S. magazines in English-language bookstores, but the cost is higher than in the States.

Book Buying

English-language bookstores include both American and British books. Paris offers the most varied selection, but most large cities will offer some English-language books. Here are a few bookstores or general merchandise stores that offer books in English.

Abbey Bookshop. This small but service-oriented store supplies books from Canada, Ireland, the U.S., and the U.K. It has a literary emphasis with a quick-order service for popular titles. Open Monday through Saturday, 10 a.m. to 7 p.m. Location: 29, rue Parcheminerie 75005 Paris; *Métro*: St-Michel; telephone: 01 46 33 16 24 or 01 40 46 07 07; fax: 01 46 33 03 33; website: *http://ourworld.compuserve.com/homepages/ABParis.*

Albion. Carries British and American literature and some nonfiction. Open Monday through Saturday; hours vary, depending on season from 9:30 or 10:30 a.m. to 6 or 7 p.m. Location: 13, rue Charles V, 75004 Paris; *Métro*: St. Paul; telephone: 01 42 72 50 71.

American University of Paris Bookstore. Open to those affiliated with the American University. Specializes in academic and reference books. Location: 10, bis rue Amélie, 75007 Paris; telephone: 02 40 62 05 92.

Brentano's. This large and active American bookstore carries best-sellers, nonfiction, children's books, magazines, and newspapers. Services include international magazine subscriptions, mail-order books, and special events. Open Monday through Saturday, 10 a.m. to 7:30 p.m. Location: 37, avenue de l'Opéra, 75002 Paris; *Métro*: Opéra; telephone: 01 42 61 52 50; fax: 01 42 61 07 61.

FNAC. Though not a bookstore as such, FNAC is a general entertainment store with stereo and computer equipment and other electronics—it has a large book section, mostly in French but with some English-language titles. FNAC stores are located in Paris and other major cities such as Tours.

Galignani. Carries novels, nonfiction, travel guides, and periodicals, among other things. Location: 224, rue de Rivoli, 75001 Paris; *Métro*: Tuileries; telephone: 01 42 60 76 07; fax: 01 42 86 09 31; e-mail: *galignan@imaginet.fr.*

San Francisco Book Co. An American and English secondhand bookshop. Open Monday to Saturday, 11 a.m. to 9 p.m. and Sunday, 2 to 9 p.m. Location: 17, rue Monsieur le Prince, 75006 Paris; *Métro*: Odéon; telephone: 01 43 29 15 70; fax: 01 43 29 52 48; e-mail: *sfbooks@easynet.fr.*

Shakespeare & Company. An absent-minded-professor-style store, where shelves are packed in a fascinating chaos of floor-to-ceiling books. Open daily, noon to midnight. Location: 37, rue de la Bucherie, 75005 Paris; *Métro:* St. Michel; telephone: 01 43 26 96 50.

Tea and Tattered Pages. Here you'll find used books galore in mostly paperback form with some hardcover and collector's items. A trading operation lets you sell your used paperbacks for two to five francs, then save ten percent off your next used paperback purchase. Open seven days a week, from 11 a.m. to 7 p.m. Location: 24, rue Mayet, 75006 Paris; *Métro:* Duroc; telephone: 01 40 65 94 35; fax: 01 30 21 97 36.

Village Voice. Literary bookstore where you can find contemporary fiction and poetry, plus serious nonfiction, such as philosophy. Presents free readings and events. Open Tuesday to Saturday, 10 a.m. to 8 p.m.; Sunday and Monday, 2 to 8 p.m. Location: 6, rue Princesse, 75006 Paris; *Métro:* Mabillon; telephone: 01 46 33 36 47; fax: 01 46 33 27 48; website: *http://www.paris-anglo.com.*

Virgin Megastore. The main store is on the Champs-Elysées, with a kiosk at the Louvre mall. Offers a large selection of English and French books, as well as records and CDs. Main location: 52, avenue des Champs-Elysées, 75008 Paris; telephone: 01 49 53 50 00.

WH Smith. A glossy, bright English bookstore just around the corner from the U.S. embassy near the Concorde. English and American fiction and nonfiction and children's books, magazines, newspapers, audio/video cassettes, and CD-ROM. Hosts book signings and events. Location: 248, rue de Rivoli, 75001 Paris; *Métro:* Concorde; telephone: 01 44 77 88 99; fax: 01 42 96 83 71; e-mail: *WHSmith.france@wanadoo.fr.*

Locations Hither and On-line. It's tougher to find English-language books outside Paris, but not impossible. Small English-language bookstores exist in most large cities. Or, a shelf or rack may be devoted to English-language books in large bookstores.

French libraries often have an English-language section for students and customers who want the practice—or for those of us English speakers who want simply to relax with a book that doesn't require constant use of a dictionary!

Don't forget the Internet. You can order books on-line through *www.Amazon.com* (U.S.-based) or *www.Amazon.co.uk* (British-based) Other sites include *www.acses.com,* which lets you compare prices and search for books. At *www.1Bookstreet.com* you will not be charged for shipping, but books are sent parcel post rather than priority mail, so it takes longer to receive them.

Stroll the *Bouquinistes*

The sidewalks lining the Seine are packed spine-to-spine with book stalls, whose sellers are called *bouquinistes*. (Another word for book in French is *bouquin*.) You can find antique or just plain old books, calendars, back issues of *Paris Match* and other magazines, along with some tourist fodder, such as postcards and plastic Eiffel Towers. It's fun to peruse the offerings on a sunny day.

Books to Borrow

One way to cut the high cost of books is to borrow them from various sources. Get your loaners from:

The American Library in Paris. This is a treasure trove with the largest selection of English-language books in Paris. Events are held periodically, so it's also the start of a social life for bookworms. You can join for four or six months to try it, or a full year. Individual rates are 240 FF ($40), 350 FF ($58), and 570 FF ($95) respectively. Also available is an annual family rate of 790 FF ($132) and an annual student rate of 460 FF ($77). Location: 10, rue du Général-Camou, 75007 Paris; *Métro*: Alma-Marceau; telephone: 01 53 59 12 60.

Library of the American University of Paris. Thousands of titles are available but only for students and faculty members at the American University of Paris. (Sadly, the former agreement for use by members of The American Library is no longer in effect.) Location: 9, rue de Montessuy, 75007 Paris; *Métro*: Alma-Marceau; telephone 01 40 62 05 57.

Trading Pages. Get friendly with other English speakers, and you'll find that the book trade is a popular activity. Be sure to put your name in any books you want back, because they may travel the community before finding their way back to you.

Hobbies

Most hobbies you can indulge in the States, you can practice in France as well. Art is a major source of enjoyment, and you'll have opportunities to take lessons, if you wish, or join a group of local artists for creative outings and shows. Amateur and professional groups are active in arranging art shows where you'll see your work in a gallerylike setting. As artist or friend of an artist, you'll be invited to the opening (*vernissage*). At the least, you'll enjoy the art and a glass of wine.

Photography is not as popular as fine art in France, but photo clubs operate in the larger towns; you can, with a little searching, find darkrooms to rent. If you belong to a photo club, they usually have available darkrooms for members and have arranged for a member discount with a local supplier for your developing, paper, chemicals, and other necessities. Sometimes it's worth the membership fee just to get the discount, even if you don't participate in the club's events.

ENTERTAINMENT

Movies

If you understand French a little, you can enjoy movies for the action and use them as practice in comprehending the language. Pick a movie you'd enjoy and go for the visuals and whatever you can grasp. If you can't handle that, look for an English-language film at a theater that plays foreign films in the original language with French subtitles. American and British films will, of course, be in English. Just look for the words *Version Originale*, or more often, the initials *VO* in the newspaper listing or on the movie poster.

In Paris you'll have no problem finding original-language films; theaters that play them line the Champs-Elysées. Other large towns will often have a theater that plays some original-language movies. Even our small town of 3,500 people has designated Tuesday as original-language night. (Of course, on the first three Tuesdays, the films were Belgian, Italian, and Chinese. Yes, they were in the original language, which was not English.)

Theaters are modern or jury-rigged, depending on the size of the town, but you may be surprised. That movie theater behind the eighteenth-century facade will most likely have been updated with comfortable, staged seating and up-to-date screens and sound systems. Major theaters will serve candy and popcorn. Smaller ones may not have anything on offer, or may, like our favorite, serve *quiche* in their café before or after the movie.

Tickets cost about 45 FF ($7.50); they're often discounted on Mondays and sometimes on Wednesdays. Students and children get discounts. Many theaters also have a subscription program. If you join, you get a discount and a copy of the film magazine and schedule mailed to you regularly. Check the movie listings for particulars.

Videos

You can rent or purchase movies and entertainment videos, though the majority are in French. Large stores and English-language bookstores may offer English-language films, especially in Paris. Your video player from the States won't work in France, so you'll have to have a French model (see page 80). However, if you want to watch videos from the U.S., you can buy a video player that will play both types.

Live Entertainment

Plays are difficult to enjoy, unless your French is exceptionally good. But you can find concerts ranging from jazz to classical to hip hop. Watch for posters or local advertising. An evening jazz concert with a river and lighted *château* as a backdrop is a superb experience.

Television

France offers five public television channels, though you may need cable or a satellite dish to pick them up well. Television does offer an inexpensive learning experience (see page 32).

Other than that, just pick programs you would enjoy in English, even if they're dubbed. *X-Files* plays here and Mulder and Scully speak perfect French.

To pick up English-language shows, you'll need to have a satellite dish or cable. The free or inexpensive choices in English include CNN, CNBC, EuroSport, BBC News, Sky News, the Cartoon Channel, and Turner Network. Our French improved more quickly before we moved to the house with a satellite dish, which tempted us to watch English-language programming now and then.

Movie channels are available but are pricey, so it depends on what you're willing to pay. You'll also get channels in Spanish, German, Italian, Polish, Portuguese, and other languages from locations all around Europe. Late at night, you can flip to some channels that will steam up your screen. This is good or bad news, depending on your tastes, but just be aware, especially if there are children in the house.

CHEAP THRILLS

Wondering how to occupy your time without spending a fortune? That's not difficult in France. Though not averse to material pleasures, the French are not as caught up in spending as a hobby as Americans, and you'll find some simply wonderful experiences are free or low-cost. Take advantage of them.

> *Ten kilometers away, down a small side road, sits a Celtic dolmen from circa 2,500 B.C. No fences, no admission fee. Picnic table nearby, that's all.... Blows my mind just to see it!*
> —Dorothy, Haute-Savoie

Wander Flea Markets

You don't have to buy anything to enjoy the show of honest-to-goodness antiques, as well as just plain junk. (But it's interesting *French* junk!) There are permanent *brocantes* (antique markets) as well as outdoor *brocantes* that are held various days of the week. The latter can be more like a small fair, with sidewalk vendors of sausages or crêpes or wine—enough to make a whole afternoon of fun.

Sit at an Outdoor Café

For a few francs, you can sit in a sidewalk café for as long as you want. Notice that French sit facing out toward the sidewalk, all the better to view the people parade.

Walk

Pure and simple, a walk in France takes on a whole new dimension. Take bustling streets past the cultural and architectural treasures of Paris, a simple out-of-the-way village (with its fifteenth-century church), one of thousands of marked forest trails, or down a road peppered with workers gathering the grapes.

Bike

A variation of the above, but just as pleasurable. Find a good used bike, if you can. Watch local classifieds or announcement boards at grocery stores. Once you have the bike, you're free to go even farther abroad. Bike from one small town to another or along a river path.

Visit Churches

Most churches and cathedrals in France are open for your prayers and perusal—and are absolutely free. Even the old, out-of-the-way chapels are every bit as interesting as the ones you'll find in the tour books. The smallest church near us has a fifteenth-century, painted wooden statue of St. George slaying his dragon, religious oil paintings ranging from the sixteenth to nineteenth century, and an old-country stone nave that carries the charm of authenticity.

Concerts

Watch for notices of concerts in churches, galleries, outdoor terraces, and town halls. These are often free or inexpensive, especially in summer, when restaurants or municipalities underwrite the entertainment to attract tourists.

Visit Art Shows

Art galleries and art shows are open to the public. The opening nights may be closed to the public; but, as mentioned earlier, if you or your friends have art in the show, you will be invited to the social occasion. Go and mingle and practice your French.

And one of the least known, but best deals ever...

Les Journées du Patrimoine

Once a year, a special weekend (usually the third weekend in September) is designated *Les Journées du Patrimoine*. On this weekend, many of France's national treasures are open to the public for free or at a special reduced rate. Sometimes the sites offer a *visite insolite*, which is an unusual tour that goes behind-the-scenes to areas not normally open to the public. At the *Château de Blois*, we passed behind inconspicuous doors to hidden corridors and stairs for a free two-hour tour of the sixteenth-century attics and cellars that we never would have seen any other time of year.

LE BON MOT: ENTERTAINING WORDS

Actualités	News
Bibliothèque	Library
Brocante	Flea market
Chaine	Channel (TV)
Cinéma	Movie theater
Film	Movie
Galerie	Gallery
Librairie	Bookstore
Musée	Museum
Spectacle	Show
Vernissage	Art-show opening
Version originale	Original-language version

18
Shopping Sprees

ONE MUST CHOOSE, IN LIFE, BETWEEN MAKING MONEY
AND SPENDING IT. THERE IS NO TIME TO DO BOTH.
—Edouard Bourdet, *Les Temps Difficiles*

As an American, shopping is a hobby, albeit one that I was glad to put on the back burner, in order to enjoy a new lifestyle in France. Our own sojourn was made possible by tightening the *ceinture* a bit, rather than buying a new one. However, there does come a time when one needs to shop for something—be it a new sweater, shoes, or a coffee maker for the kitchen.

France offers a range of shops, from small boutique operations to large chain stores. The range of products is vast but not nearly as large as what Americans are accustomed too. Still, you won't lack for possibilities for spending your money.

OPEN SIGNS AND OTHER BASICS

Shopping hours range widely in France, because stores tend to be independent in their thinking. The area where you live plays a big part in whether you can shop at 10 at night or Sundays. For the most part, general-merchandise stores in France open from about 9 or 9:30 a.m. to 12 or 12:30 p.m. Stores reopen from 2 or 2:30 p.m. to 7 or 7:30. Large department stores in Paris and other big cities usually stay open through the lunch hour. In small towns, the stores often close *en masse* for one day a week. Ours close on Tuesdays, and anyone stopping by main street would think it was a ghost town except for the smells wafting from the one *boulangerie* that stays open that day and closes Wednesday.

The variety of hours and closing times means that you must learn the specific hours of the shops you patronize, or you will face what we did for the first six months; we confused which ones were open through lunch and which ones weren't, resulting in wasted trips to malls or long lunches waiting for shops to reopen.

In general, small, local stores have more limited opening hours than larger stores. Your local tradespeople own the store, and they work it themselves with the help of family and the occasional employee. It's impossible for them to be in the store around the clock. There's that long lunch, remember? They can't be there every month, either because there are *les vacances* to consider. And when their children have a special event at school, well, sorry, but the shop's closed, even if you did want that lamp today.

On one magnificent day in spring, the sun blasted down after weeks of gloomy skies. Passing through town at 3 p.m. I noticed that the local mattress-seller had posted a sign in the window: "*Je suis a l'Esperance.*" If anyone wanted him, he was available, but he obviously wasn't going to waste a beautiful day inside, when he could be sitting under a café umbrella.

Comparison Shopping

As you become accustomed to the French franc, you can begin serious comparison shopping. Then you'll discover which stores offer the most value. You'll also learn when to shop the sales.

Like the variety of merchandise itself, sales are bigger and better in the larger commercial centers in France. There's simply more competition. In smaller towns, such as mine, the prices may be higher, though the convenience is often worth it. When we bought our VCR, it was a few francs more in the shop near our home. But knowing our inability to program a VCR, even in English, we bought it locally and *Monsieur* set it up for us.

We patronized so many of the local merchants for other purchases that, at the town's welcoming ceremony for new residents, the room was packed with people we knew. We're sure this helped establish us as people who were already part of the community. And the smiles we got from merchants were wider the following week.

Paying the Cashier

The salesperson in a large store, and sometimes in smaller ones, is often not the person who accepts the payment. This is a nice touch that separates that nasty money issue from the salesperson's help.

When you've made a selection at a store, you may be requested to pay for it at the *caisse*. Large stores take major charge cards, such as Visa,

MasterCard, American Express, and the Carte Bleu debit card, though there's often a minimum of 100 francs for charges.

If you don't receive a receipt, ask for a *ticket*. (That's pronounced *tee-kay*.)

Value-Added Tax (VAT)

The *Taxe à la Valeur Ajoutée* (TVA) in French is what the English would call the Value-Added Tax, or VAT for short. This tax, between 18.6 and 33 percent, is added to the cost of many items you buy, not just in France but throughout Europe. The tax is not added to food or wine, by the way, since the French understand that these are the true necessities of life.

Tourists can fill out a VAT refund form, which major stores will provide at the time of purchase. It's stamped by customs officials when leaving the country. When the stamped form is sent to the store, a refund is mailed via check (in foreign currency) or is credited to the credit card used, if the item was charged.

Of course, living in France means you don't leave, or at least not often enough to get VAT credit. It's even a problem with other countries you visit. When we took the ferry to Ireland from France and back to France, we joyfully figured the tax savings on all those lovely Irish wool sweaters we'd splurged on. It wasn't until the eleventh hour of the eighteen-hour ferry ride back that we realized we had to leave the European Union to get the credit.

FAMOUS FRENCH CRAFTS AND WHERE TO FIND THEM

China.	Limoges
	Quimper
	Sèvres
Knives	Languiole
Lace.	Bretagne
Antiques	*Brocantes* can be found anywhere, though the less they've been picked over by tourists, the better.
Perfumes.	Grasse
High fashion.	Paris
Lavender	Provence
Crystal.	Baccarat

Types of Stores

Small and Specialty Shops

In France many of the stores are not just Mom-and-Pop stores, they're Grandma-and-Grandpa stores. Shop owners often live in their community for years, and their businesses have been passed down from one generation to the next.

This personal ownership enables the owners to know their regular customers, and they respond accordingly. If you work the system well, you'll enjoy personal attention beyond your dreams, with service and advice worthy of royalty. The opposite can also be true, as you, a foreigner, may be seen as a mere tourist. You'll be waited on, often pleasantly, but nothing extra will be forthcoming. Your objective in the small local stores, whether hardware store, clothing store, or a newsstand, is to build a relationship, just as you did with the baker and butcher.

Because these small shops are individually (often family) owned, it's important to be polite when entering one. Recognize the salesperson with a *"bonjour"* and take into account that the owner's pride and joy are on the shelves. Be more hesitant than you would in Wal-Mart of pawing through those neat stacks of sweaters. In the typical small shop, the items are on display, and the salesperson will help you. In larger stores, serve-it-yourself may or may not be expected. You'll know the difference.

Mega Stores

Chain stores abound in France, especially in and around large cities. Among the more popular names you'll notice are *Auchan, Continent, BricoMarché, Vetimarché,* and *Intermarché.*

A major appliance chain in France is Darty, which is actually British in origin. The store covers its products with excellent warranty service, and you can request an additional discount if you buy several items at once.

You can find anything you really need in France, though under different brands. If, by any chance, you don't find something you desperately need that is American in origin, you can always try Stateside Online Shopping. It's an Internet-based shopping service for military personnel, diplomats, or anyone living abroad. They'll purchase and ship you the item you want for a fee. It might be necessary in Timbuktu, but shouldn't be necessary in France. However, if you're interested, contact *http://www.stateside-shopping.com/.*

We didn't know how to dress, at first, for what the French called a casual party.
With the other Americans, we can just wear jeans, but the French idea
of casual is three notches higher.
—John, Loire Valley

BEING IN FASHION

Clothes in France, the high-fashion capital of the world, are for the normal American woman, a disappointment. Frankly, you'll be hard-pressed to find clothes that are of the quality Americans are accustomed to for similar prices. The fabrics tend to be thinner with less body to them; this is especially true of cottons.

However, the French are very much aware of their appearance and tend to dress more formally than the average American. French women bike or totter merrily down cobblestone streets in heels, never dreaming of wearing sneakers unless they're on a tennis court. Our next-door neighbor rakes her flower beds in a neat skirt, sweater set, and mid-size black heels, while I hide behind a tree in my scruffy sweat pants.

Sophisticated Parisians buy the best clothes they can afford, in classic styles that stay in fashion *toujours*. The rakishly tied scarf is still a symbol of French fashion after decades, and no proper French woman would be without a wardrobe of them.

The best places to find clothes are in larger cities and big stores, where you'll find a much greater variety and sometimes better quality than in the countryside. Department stores, such as *Le Printemps* and *Samaritaine*, offer a wide range of clothes for the family, plus household items. They're located in Paris, with branches in other large cities. Seek out specialty boutiques for sizes that are larger or smaller than normal, and for more sophisticated fashions. One fashion store that's known for stylish clothes at low prices is *Tati*, which has several stores around Paris and branches in other cities.

You'll recognize many brand names in France, where Benetton, Burberry, Jaeger, and Levi's (both the brand name and jeans knock-offs) are popular. Levi's, by the way, are found all over, but are more expensive than in the United States. Jeans are one thing that most American expats put on the shopping list on a visit back to the States.

Shoes are priced comparably to those in the States, but do not come in half-sizes. Check the size chart to find the closest size.

> *I don't [usually] buy clothes here, but I did buy a cocktail dress. Everyone and their brother was right outside the dressing room, having things altered in some way. You can't be shy.*
>
> —Pam, Le Mans

Sizing Up the Situation

Even if you limit your croissant intake, your size expands considerably in France. A woman who wears a size 8 in the United States, wears a French size 38. A man's U.S. 16-neck shirt is a French size 40. This is all very disheartening to anyone who enjoys bragging about their svelte waist. The only solution is to figure out your size for purchases, then don't look at the label afterwards.

Following is a list of U.S.-to-French size conversions. This will give you a starting point for when you begin looking through the clothing racks; sizes don't exactly match up so you'll have to experiment. As in any clothes shopping, the perfect fit will depend on the style and the manufacturer's cut.

WOMEN'S CLOTHES CONVERSIONS

Dresses

France	U.S.	British
36	6	28
38	8	30
40	10	32
42	12	34
44	14	36
46	16	38
48	18	40
50	20	42

Sweaters/Blouses

France	U.S.	British
38	32	32
40	34	34
42	36	36
44	38	38
46	40	40
48	42	42

Women's Shoes

France	U.S.	Britain
36	5	3
37	6	4
38	7	5
39	7.5	6
40	8	7
41	9	8

MEN'S CLOTHES CONVERSIONS

Men's Shirts

France	U.S.
36	14
37	$14^1/_2$
38	15
39	$15^1/_2$
40	16
41	$16^1/_2$
42	17
43	$17^1/_2$
44	18

Men's Suits

France	U.S.	Britain
36	35	35
38	36	36
40	37	37
42	38	38
44	39	39
46	40	40
48	42	42

Men's Shoes

France	U.S.	Britain
41	8	8
42	$8^1/_2$	9
43	$9^1/_2$	10
44	10	11
45	$10^1/_2$	12
46	11	13

Children's Clothes Conversions

In America, baby clothes sizes are based on age—six months, a year, and eighteen months, for example—which doesn't provide much help, since babies of the same age come in all sizes. The same is true in France for young children's clothes. The only solution is to check the measurements and try everything on the child.

LE BON MOT: CLOTHING TERMS

Chaussures. . . . . Shoes
Costume . . . . Suit (men's)
Gilet. . . . . Jacket
Jupe. . . . . Skirt
Manteau . . . . Coat
Pantalons. . . . . Trousers
Robe. . . . . Dress
Tailleur . . . . Suit (women's)

...and one very important word...
Solde . . . . Sale!

19
Vacationing–Oops–Working in France

THE ONLY WAY ANYBODY'D GET ME TO WORK WAS TO MAKE THE HOURS
FROM ONE TO TWO WITH AN HOUR OFF FOR LUNCH.
—Minnesota Fats, pool hustler

Between the six weeks of vacation, Christmas and New Year's weeks, Easter, Bastille Day, Labor Day, Armistice Day, plus sundry other holidays and saints' days, and lunches that last three hours, it's not long before Americans working in France begin to feel they're not working at all.

It's not completely fun and games, of course. French workers often return from that long lunch to work until seven or eight that evening. I have it on good authority that Parisians may even—horrors—skip the long lunch and down a quick *sandwich* while running errands.

Overall, though, the average person working in France avoids that intense, unremitting stress, and does not face what Americans seem to have invented: burnout. Relaxing lunches and regular holidays provide the chance to recuperate and regenerate their energy.

All this culminates in the month-long holiday, *les vacances*, which is traditionally taken in August, though some people are now taking it in July. For those traditional leave-takers, there's more stress getting to the holiday spot on the French roads than in actually working. The national French news programs have special maps, similar to weather maps, but noting the traffic jams. I don't know that it helps. Everyone seems to leave Paris like lemmings on the same day, at the same hour. No one wants to waste one precious minute, so they all leave immediately following the last day of work in July, which means that trips start at a dead stop on the *autoroute*...but they're *en vacances* with everyone else in France, and that's what counts.

How do you work yourself into the situation of workers, who love their work *and* their play?

WORKING CONDITIONS

Full-time workers in France enjoy not only long vacations but also good employment conditions and social security benefits. French labor regulations set minimum employment conditions, such as working hours, overtime, holidays, and dismissal regulations. The minimum wage is 40,22 FF or $6.70 an hour, but taxes reduce the actual take-home pay considerably.

Employees are covered under employment contracts, which indicate each party's responsibilities regarding the job, from title and salary to benefits and working hours. There are contracts for indefinite and definite terms plus seasonal and temporary work, and these contracts are renewable, though each party must agree. A contract may be for the duration of just a month, for example, then renewed for another month. A full-time, professional-level job might start with a year contract. If you're a worker applying for a residence permit, you must show your employment contract.

Full-time employees get five weeks' vacation (*vacances*) each year or more. Most people take four of them during the summer, usually in July and August. Some companies just give up the ghost entirely and rather than try to operate with a skeleton staff, they close completely during the month of August. The second most popular vacation time for a week or so, is during the winter for a ski holiday or getaway to a sunny location.

Maternity leaves (*congé maternité*) are generous, with sixteen weeks off at full pay in addition to the five weeks' vacation. This, of course, only comes if you are already working in the French social security system.

For the most part, workers also get public holidays off. These include Christmas and New Year's, as well as various religious holidays and war remembrances. The list includes:

January 1	New Year's Day/*Nouvel An*
March/April	Easter Monday/*Lundi de Pâques*
May 1	Labor Day/*Fête du Travail*
May 8	Victory Day/*Fête de la Libération*
May	Ascension Day/*Ascension*
May/June	Pentecost/*Pentecôte*
July 14	Bastille Day/*Fête Nationale*
August 15	Assumption/*l'Assomption*
November 1	All Saints' Day/*Toussaint*
November 11	Armistice Day/*l'Armistice*
December 25	Christmas/*Noël*

Often when a holiday falls on a Tuesday or Thursday, a "bridge" or *pont* is created, giving the Monday before or the Friday after the holiday off as well.

> *Now that they have the 35-hour week, Steve has to take*
> *two extra days a month off. The work police check parking lots to see*
> *whose cars stay more than thirty-five hours, and they can fine companies.*
> *For someone in his position, it's impossible [to get the work done].*
> *But he can take one a month and "bank" it.*
> *Some year, we'll take a year off!*
> —Pam, Le Mans

Sécurité Sociale

Every worker, even foreign employees and the self-employed, must contribute to the social security system (*sécurité sociale*), which provides extensive benefits in pensions, health care, and unemployment. Many companies also offer additional health insurance that picks up where the *sécurité sociale* leaves off.

The official French retirement age is sixty for men and women, although with the growing problems in unemployment, some companies and unions are negotiating for earlier retirements (*pré-retraite*).

> *We paid into the French Social Security while my husband was working here,*
> *and it's a very high rate. But now we're set with the pension*
> *and one hundred percent health-care coverage.*
> —Sara, the Ardèche

Taxes—the Plus and Minus

Taking a job in France, either full-time or part-time, will enmesh you in the French tax system, which is very steep and complicated. A person living in France and working for a French company is considered to have his tax domicile in France. You are considered a resident for tax purposes if your main country of residence is France, and you spend more than 183 days in France during the calendar year.

If you work in France, you will need to register with the local tax authorities (*Centre des Imports*) when you arrive. Nonresidents of France are taxed only on their income in France.

U.S. Social Security Regulations

If you're receiving U.S. Social Security but want to work in France, you will be subject to a work/time test. Overseas regulations are different, and the Social Security Administration does not consider you retired if you work part-time more than forty-five hours a month. If you intend to work part-time, check the current regulations to avoid losing part of your Social Security benefits.

Cheer Up...Consider This Tax Exclusion

The U.S. taxes nonresident citizens on worldwide income; however, working in France (or anywhere overseas, for that matter) provides the possibility of a $70,000 exclusion on foreign-earned income. The exclusion applies to each spouse, so if a couple works overseas, they may exclude up to $140,000. You may still have to pay taxes in France, which are among the highest in the world, but this exclusion lessens the blow.

The best advice? Talk to a professional tax adviser before taking the job, to ensure that you arrange the best situation for your specific situation and finances.

Working on a student visa is easier [than getting a work visa]....
I know people who have student visas even though they're in their thirties,
one's forty even. It's a different kind of contract.

—Cary, Pau

FINDING A JOB

Don't go to France expecting to find a job easily—or of finding a job at all. The country's high unemployment rate means that anyone entering the country to work is instantly suspect, and getting a work permit is extremely difficult.

One way to get full-time work in France is to have your present company transfer you. One man learned of an opening in the Le Mans office, and before you could say *fromage*, he'd volunteered. His wife was ready for an adventure, and after a one-week visit to see the new community, they leapt at the chance to move. If you work for a company with international connections, ask the personnel department about the possibility of overseas transfer. Learning French will increase your chances.

You can also look for a new job, though realize that there's a lot of competition. Again, you'll have an automatic leg up if you speak French. This is true even if you're working with an American company, since you'll be working in France and will need to function on a daily basis. It also shows the seriousness of your intent and desire to transfer to France.

Hundreds of U.S. companies operate, to some extent, in France. Some, but by no means all of them, include IBM, Texas Instruments, UPS, Federal Express, Chase Manhattan, and many other U.S.-based financial institutions, as well as airlines and hospitality services. Resorts and hotels use full-time personnel as well as seasonal employees. Usually they use French people, but occasionally you may find a company that needs native English-speaking people to deal with their English-speaking tourists. For lists of American companies with foreign branches, check the *Directory of American Firms Operating in Foreign Countries.*

Don't forget government and nonprofit entities based in the United States but working in France. They use English-speaking personnel.

It's very difficult to come over here to work. When the company wants you, they [will secure] the work permit. I don't know that you can do it alone.

—Melanie, Pau

Locating Want Ads

Classified ads in the *International Herald Tribune* usually feature the high-status, high-pay positions. You can also review the classifieds in large metropolitan papers, though overseas positions will be fewer by far.

FUSAC (*France-USA Contacts*) magazine has help-wanted and job-seeker columns. Most of these are for lower-end jobs, with restaurant and bar servers being among the most popular offerings. However, you'll find other positions in the list, including marketing, secretarial, and teaching English.

The term "EMT" stands for English Mother Tongue. That's you.

Classifieds in the *Paris Free Voice* tend to be along the same line as *FUSAC*, with a few "model" and "hostess" positions thrown in for good measure.

Of course, you can check local papers. From an American point of view, ads in French classifieds are blatantly discriminatory with regard to age and sex. They request certain ages or levels of experience that are, often under age thirty-five with from two to seven years' work experience, meaning they want someone who's wet behind the ears but who they can expect to have energy and work with them long enough to justify the time in training.

Responding to Want Ads

In Europe resumes are called *curriculum vitae* (CV, for short). State your proficiency in French on the CV, noting if it's good (*bien*), very good (*trés bien*), fluent (*courant*), or mother tongue (*langue maternelle*)—if you were lucky enough to have a French parent or lived in France as a child.

When responding to a want ad, you may also be requested to send a handwritten letter, not a typed one. This is due to the fact that some employers in France use graphology to analyze their candidates' writing. This is becoming less common in recent years, however. You may also be requested to send a photograph.

If you write a French letter, follow French conventions for business letters, which are more formal than U.S. letters. Books are available in French libraries and bookstores that provide formats for business correspondence.

On-Line Searches

The World Wide Web puts a world of job openings at your fingertips. Use it to do preliminary research on international companies and even to find specific jobs. Hundreds of sites cover various fields. Among them are the following:

Career Guide. Used by top international recruiters and business schools. Website: *http://www.career-guide.com.*

CareerMosaic. This gateway leads to various sites that pertain to international jobs in particular, and job-search tips in general. Includes job listings, employer profiles, and resume-posting sections. Website: *http://www.careermosaic.com.*

Career Path. Links to job pages in almost ninety U.S. newspapers, which means most of the jobs are in the States. Jobs are also gathered from the Web, which broadens the possibilities. Also provides company profiles, resume-posting, and other tips. Website: *http://www.CareerPath.com.*

Career Web. Offers classifieds, resume postings, and job matching. Website: *http://www.careerweb.com.*

EMDS. Organizes MBA and career events worldwide and provides MBA grads with opportunity to meet leading European and international employers. Website: *http://www.emdsnet.com.*

Jobware. An excellent site for international and national job searches. Clients include major companies, and offers are listed in various languages, for various countries. Website: *http://www.jobware.net.*

Monster Job Board. Allows you to check jobs overseas by clicking "International" under "Career Zones," then to narrow your search to France. Website: *http://www.monster.com.*

Overseas Jobs. Just what the title indicates: specializes in jobs abroad. Website: *http://www.overseasjobs.com.*

> *I was lucky enough to enter a yearlong training program for guide-interpreters, but it's hard for most guides to find full-time work. My wife is French, so I got a work permit. And I speak French well, so I'm able to lead English-speaking and French tourists, which is a plus.*
> —Scott, Orléans

How to Boost Your Odds of Finding Work

Learn French

This may seem obvious, but some people assume that, if they're looking for a job with an American company, they can just learn when they arrive. You'll have to deal with an international community and, if you already speak credible French, it not only proves you to be a practical asset, but enhances your standing as a person who is serious about living and working in France.

Network Internationally

Become involved in groups promoting French language and culture. Alliance Française offers more than language classes. It also presents art exhibits, cultural events, and social gatherings.

Offer a Skill

Be prepared with solid skills. If you can program computers or are an expert at marketing, an American-style skill that's admired in France lately, you may be on track for a job offer.

Show Initiative

People do work in France with and without work permits. They have one thing in common: initiative and the willingness to open their minds to new kinds of work or self-employment.

Work Permitting

An American who wants to work in France must have a work permit. As mentioned, this is difficult to get, since the French unemployment rate is around ten percent. Chances are you won't be working for an French firm, so I won't go into the numerous regulations and French tax and social security implications. If you go this route, you'll need the specialized attention of tax and financial advisers, and the company that hires you will hopefully help sort things out. Most companies and all temporary agencies require you to have a work permit, based on your visa, before they'll take you as a client.

An EU Passport Opens the Door

Some countries, including Ireland and Italy, have regulations that permit a person with close ancestors there (for example, a grandfather born in Ireland) to apply for a passport from that country. You do not lose your American citizenship. You do get an avenue by which you can enter into France as a legal passport-holding member of the European Union, with fewer restrictions on working than your American passport provides.

Working Around the Permit

If you can't work officially, what can you do to earn a living while in France? One option is to work for yourself in a consultant, freelance, or creative endeavor. If you are a permanent resident with the *carte de résident*, you can be self-employed officially, but as an American (non-EU), you must obtain that residence permit. That's the sticky part. There are three classes of self-employed: professionals, merchants, and craftsmen. There are many other regulations and, if you want to officially start a business, then you will have to bone up on them. However, some people quietly run small home-based businesses to bypass the bureaucracy.

Menial positions occasionally (very occasionally) can be found working for an individual who pays you "under the counter," such as when a farmer or vintner needs workers quickly. (As for the latter case, in many areas the traditional grape harvest is mechanized, so this is becoming rarer.) In any case, without good French and local connections, it isn't likely you'll find much work. Here are a few other ideas that may be more interesting and less backbreaking.

Welcome Other Americans

A couple in the Loire Valley bought several old farm buildings, which are now charming rental properties. They rent them out to other Americans via friends of friends or carefully selected advertising in the United States. The husband also hires himself out as a contractor to supervise improvements on other American's dreams when they can't or don't want to be in France to manage the workmen themselves.

Be Artistic

The creative field is ripe in this cultural country, which has attracted writers and artists for centuries. The likes of Ernest Hemingway, Gertrude Stein, and Alice B. Toklas made Paris their cultural hometown, while F. Scott Fitzgerald found the posh Riviera more to his liking. Today, both the city and the country are teeming with wannabe artists and novelists who've been joined by web designers and cartoonists, cookbook authors, and travel writers, all of whom have made their work transportable.

Work in the States (Live in France)

These days, with computers and e-mail and Fed Ex and faxes, you can live virtually anywhere. Many marketing and sales personnel use France as a base, but sell their products elsewhere. Some keep companies set up in the States, working as "consultants" in France. The fees are paid to the companies in the States, not to the person in France. Strange bedfellows can be created this way. As an example: I write a newsletter via the Internet for an ad agency in Atlanta, whose client is a German company. Yes, it's complicated, but if it works, then you do too!

I went to our *mairie* and asked [about a license to open a bed and breakfast]. They never heard of such a thing and sent me to the *mairie* in the large town nearby. They never heard of it either and sent me to the *sous-préfecture*. The woman serving me hadn't any idea what I was talking about but got out a gigantic ledger and offered me a choice of four different restaurant and bar licenses, none of which was appropriate and all of which had to be paid for.

Fortunately, I knew what I wanted, and so returned home empty-handed again. Finally I called the *préfecture* in the departmental capital. They told me to call the tax office. There a very nice man said it wasn't his area of expertise....His colleague was, of course, on holiday. But he would return in ten days.

I went to the local tax office and met the man. "Oh, yes," he smiled, "I have it right here in this drawer!" No, he didn't. Out of stock. Before I could start crying, he brightened up and asked, "Do you know Mme. Begou?"

"You mean Mme. Begou, who owns the *tabac* in our village?"

"Yes," he said, "she has them."

And she did.

—Margo, Rémuzat, the Drôme Provençale

Teach English

France is obviously closer to England than it is to the United States, so most of the language training is undertaken in the King's English. As an American, you can teach English, but target the individuals and schools that concentrate on American-style English. Berlitz is one of these schools, although there are many others. Check their ads or call the schools near you, to see which style of English they teach.

Some schools teach the general public and others specialize in teaching English to businesspeople. Lessons for the latter group are held individually or in small groups at offices or private homes. Check the yellow pages under *Enseignements: langues.* To teach English formally, you'll need a bachelor of arts degree, and it helps to have a TEFL (Teaching English as a Foreign Language) certificate, though you may be able to use other training or experience to get your foot in the door.

In Paris check the classifieds in the *Paris Free Voice, FUSAC,* and local papers. Check job boards at the American Church. In the countryside, there will be fewer formal schools, but contact the local primary school and ask if they need someone locally. Another option is to put your own ad in the local paper or on bulletin boards.

Translate/Consult/Edit

Businesses or sites that cater to English-speaking tourists or other businesses need translations. If your French (and English) is good enough, you may find work as a translator. Or you can work in partnership with a translator to edit their literal words into smoother English.

Major companies and business schools host seminars that teach incoming executives the culture and customs of France. Once you're familiar with the country, you can develop your own program to present or offer yourself as a seminar leader.

Represent Yourself

Is there a company in your hometown that needs a representative in France? Since you'll be there anyway, perhaps you could work out a small retainer or work on commission. Or could you represent your American city or town as a cultural ambassador to promote the city to French businesses or tourists?

Start a Company

In France, a limited liability corporation is called a *SARL* or *Société à Responsabilité Limitée*. I mention this only because it's another possibility and, in certain situations, it may work for you. However, a formal company will embroil you in the French bureaucracy, taxes, and countless other complications.

My personal feeling is that moving to France should allow one the time to actually appreciate the surroundings and opportunities. Think long and hard before starting a formal business entity. If you do decide to start a company, consult experts on all the ramifications.

Lead Tours

U.S.-based tour groups need leaders for both the traditional tours as well as sport-related holidays. Bike-tour guides are especially needed these days, if you like the outdoors and can manage a group of people and their bike repairs. It's also a way for you to meet new people and travel within France.

Arrange a Seminar

Provide traveling seminars on your specialty. Set up art, cooking, photography, writing, or historic tours of France for other Americans or English speakers on vacation. You can market yourself via hometown groups, schools, classified ads, in specialty publications, and on the Internet.

Think Creatively

Consider your own skills and the work you enjoy. Make contacts wherever you can in your field and develop your own niche. It's possible to work in France, but it's not always easy. Know what you want, then research and work toward the goal before moving permanently.

Le Bon Mot: Working Words

Chef	Head officer
Contrat	Contract
Curriculum Vitae	Resume
Mi-temps	Part-time
Patron	Boss
Retraite	Retirement
Salarié	Employee
SARL (Societé à responsabilité limitée)	Corporation
Sécurité Sociale	Social Security

LIFESTYLES: ON THE FAST TRACK IN PARIS

"When I left Tennessee, little did I know that working so hard would be so much fun."

Adrian Leeds speaks quickly and enthusiastically about her new-found career. She didn't plan to work in Paris, didn't even plan to stay more than the initial year that she, her husband, and her daughter took as a sabbatical here. But they all loved France and decided to stay—though, as far as Adrian and her husband were concerned, the decision did not involve staying together.

When Adrian found herself in Paris, knowing no French, with her daughter to support, what did she do? With more energy than the Champs-Elysées lit up for Christmas, she used her marketing skills to work with other Americans to promote websites and French discussion groups. The program she began, called Parler Parlor, now counts more than 250 people, representing thirty-eight different nationalities. Each group of eight to ten people chat half the time in French, half in English, helping each other to perfect their skills in the languages. Adrian speaks French now and her daughter, she adds proudly, is completely bilingual.

"The city is alive with culture. Sure you give up the space, because apartments are so expensive, but real life is outside anyway. I know the people on my block, and it's like a small town in that way."

The American grapevine in France extends far afield, and even those who don't have official work permits seem to manage somehow in their own creativity, consulting, teaching English, or working for a French or American firm.

Do you thrive in an atmosphere bustling with possibilities, where days are filled with a cosmopolitan mix of people from around the world, along with art, music, entertainment, and a history that covers the centuries? Then you may want to join Adrian and the scores of other Americans who've brightened up their lives in the City of Light.

20
Learning through the Ages

It's virtually impossible to separate daily living from learning when you live in France. History lessons sit around every corner, in the form of Roman ruins, D-Day beaches, and caves artistically decorated by prehistoric man.

Art lessons are taught by the Louvre's grand masters, the sculptors who left their imprint on fourteenth-century cathedrals—and the local watercolor group that meets every Wednesday.

Language training is a daily round of road signs, restaurant menus, or even the telephone bill. Sociology comes as a matter of course while you learn intercultural skills at the market and attend *soirées* with new French friends.

As an adult you'll have endless opportunities for learning experiences in France, whether formal or informal. In addition, if you bring children with you, there are plenty of high-quality opportunities.

Let's take a look at various options for expanding the mind, starting with the youngest members of the family and moving up to adult courses.

Children's Schools

In France, eleven-year-olds regularly attend *collège*. No, they're not all geniuses in France. The French terms for the various school levels differ greatly from those in the United States, and their "college" isn't higher education, but rather what would be roughly equivalent to junior high in the States. Children do start school earlier, though, most at the age of three.

Here's a general breakdown of the various levels of schooling in France.

Age	School
Three to six years	*École maternelle*
Six years	*École primaire*
Seven to eight years	*Cours élémentaire*
Nine to ten years............	*Cours moyen*
Eleven to fourteen years.......	*Collège*
Fifteen to eighteen years.......	*Lycée*
Nineteen years and older	*Université* or other higher education
	Les Grand Écoles are the most prestigious

Schooling Required

French children must attend school from ages three through sixteen. Many students continue and study for the *baccalauréat* or BAC for short. This is not equivalent to the U.S. baccalaureate, in that the French BAC is only one extra year beyond a high-school diploma. However, it's an essential degree, if the student wants to gain entry into a university. Thus, a lot of pressure is put on students to pass the BAC.

Schooling is free in public schools for residents, but certain supplies are not. Parents are required to provide the usual pens and paper, and books for teenagers at *lycée* level. In primary school and *collège* the books are provided.

> Sometimes, I think that the school hours are too long.
> Our kids are often gone from 7 a.m. to 8 p.m. at night with
> one activity or another, but they do get a good education.
> As a whole, I'd rather raise kids here.
> —Scott, Orléans

School Days and Holidays

Children in France have Wednesday off, attending school Monday, Tuesday, Thursday, Friday, and Saturday mornings. Some school systems, however, are evolving into a regular Monday-through-Friday week. The school hours depend on the age of the child.

School holidays in France are not just important for children, but for adults in the surrounding community. Wednesdays, for example, are not the day to visit the mall, if you don't like hordes of kids. They're out in force on their day off.

A town's services will be based on the school holidays as well. In our town, for example, we have trouble keeping track of the indoor pool's hours, because they are based on some unfathomable schedule of school holidays based on *vacances* this and *vacances* that. For adults without school-age children, it's a mystery.

Public or Private School?

American children can either attend private international schools or the local French school. Your choice will depend on your child's ability to adapt to French, the length of time you intend to stay in France, and your budget.

Sending children to the local French school integrates them into the French culture. It enables them to meet the French children who live in the area and to adapt to the language. This is also a major drawback, however, if your child doesn't adapt quickly to learning in French.

A bilingual or international school with classes that are held in English helps children who don't know the language. However, they should be learning French at the same time. Although it's more costly, sending your child to the international school, where classes are taken in both French and English, may ease the adaptation, introduce French-language learning, and enable the child to meet different children from many different countries. When the child is conversant in French, he or she can move to the local French school.

There are many private schools in France. *The ISS Directory of Overseas Schools* by International Schools Services in Princeton, N.J., lists American and international schools worldwide, including K–12, boarding, and international baccalaureate schools.

> *Adjusting to the French education system can be tough,*
> *and I still don't agree with some of their antiquated methodology,*
> *but I've committed to seeing my daughter through high school, so she'll obtain*
> *a baccalaureate degree. That puts her two academic years ahead of her*
> *American counterparts and opens doors to universities across the globe.*
> —Adrian, Paris

Universities and Grandes Écoles

Everyone who passes the *baccalauréat* can enter a university, which explains why you'll see student protests occurring on a regular basis. The conditions at universities are not always good, with large populations of students and few professors.

You'll hear the term *Grandes Écoles*; this is not just a university but one of the most prestigious of all French educations. The *Grande Écoles* have trained most of the political and business leaders in France. Some schools specialize in engineering, sciences, or management. These schools are intensely competitive among the French and very few foreign students are admitted.

American students who want to study at French universities must have credits transferred and show original documentation of diplomas. It's much easier to enroll in one of the numerous programs in Paris, Aix-en-Provence, Toulon, and other cities that are run by American colleges with French campuses.

French consulates' cultural services departments have information on the study programs available in France. For a partial list of universities offering courses in English, see below.

Adult Education

Learning French, as discussed in chapter 4, is one of the primary learning experiences for adults living in France. You may also enjoy taking other courses or classes. If you can manage in French, various schools and organizations, such as *Accueil des Villes Françaises*, offer a range of art, craft, and language classes at moderate fees.

If you can't cope in French, look for English-speaking groups. These are particularly common in Paris, where expatriate Americans, Brits, and Australians produce courses, not only in French, but in art, sports, history, and business, among others. Many American universities run courses in France during the summer. Check *FUSAC* and *The Paris Voice* for ads that list current offerings.

General Courses

Following are just a few of the hundreds of schools and thousands of special-interest courses available in English.

The American University of Paris. This university offers adult continuing education courses in computer skills, web design, technical writing, translation, and more. Contact The Division of Continuing Education, 102, rue St. Dominique, 75007 Paris; telephone: 01 40 62 07 20; fax: 01 40 62 07 17; e-mail: *ce@aup.fr*; website: *http://www.aup.fr*.

Elderhostel. The nonprofit Elderhostel organization offers learning programs for people over fifty-five in more than seventy countries overseas, including France. The group puts out a series of catalogs for various programs. If requesting information, be sure to specify that you're interested in France. Contact Elderhostel, 75 Federal St., Boston, MA 02110-1941; website: *http://www.elderhostel.org*.

TraveLearn. Adults from age thirty to eighty can participate in learning vacations. Programs include lectures, seminars, and hands-on field experiences, without exams, grades, or attendance requirements. Contact TraveLearn, PO Box 315, Lakeville, PA 18438; telephone: (800) 235-9114; website: *http://www.travelearn.com.*

WICE. Dedicated to the English speakers in Paris, WICE offers courses and trips geared toward history, art, literature, current events, and career development. Contact WICE, 20 boulevard du Montparnasse, 75015 Paris; *Métro:* Duroc or Falguière; telephone: 01 45 66 75 50; fax: 01 40 65 96 53; e-mail : *wice@club-internet.fr.*

SPECIALIZED COURSES AND WORKSHOPS

Art & Photography

The American University of Paris. Offers arts-related classes with summer sessions. Contact The American University of Paris, 31, avenue Bosquet, 75007 Paris; telephone: 01 40 62 06 00.

The Paris American Academy. Offers programs in fine arts, fashion, and interior design. Contact Paris American Academy, 277 rue de St. Jacques, 75005 Paris; telephone: 01 44 41 99 20.

The Parsons School of Design. Classes in painting, drawing, photography, and decorative arts. Contact Parsons Paris, 14, rue Letellier, 75005 Paris; telephone: 01 45 77 39 66.

The Pont-Aven School of Art. Named for the town and artist's colony in Brittany where it's located, the school offers classes in drawing, painting, photography, and sculpture. Contact The Pont-Aven School of Art, Colline St-Guénolé, 29930 Pont-Aven; telephone: 02 98 09 10 45.

Spéos Paris Photographic Institute. Offers classes in all aspects of photography, including computer technologies, photojournalism, darkroom techniques, and much more. Contact Spéos, 7/8, rue Jules Vallès, 75011 Paris; telephone: 01 40 09 18 58; fax: 01 40 09 84 97; website: *http://www.speos.fr.*

WICE. Offers art classes among many others. Contact WICE, 20 boulevard du Montparnasse, 75015 Paris; *Métro:* Duroc or Falguière; telephone: 01 45 66 75 50; fax: 01 40 65 96 53; e-mail: *wice@club-internet.fr.*

French

Language courses and schools have already been covered in chapter 4 (page 29). Also check ads in *FUSAC,* the *Paris Voice,* or the *International Herald Tribune.*

Theater

The Cinéma Théâtre Franco-American. Bilingual workshops with individualized guidance in technique. Contact The Cinéma Théâtre Franco-American, 65, rue de Reuilly, Paris; telephone: 01 43 44 76 98.

The French-American Film Workshop. Sponsors the annual *Rencontres Cinématographiques Franco-Américaines d'Avignon,* with screenings and seminars. Contact The French-American Film Workshop, 10, Montée de la Tour, 30400 Villeneuve-les-Avignon; telephone: 04 90 25 93 23.

Food & Wine

Bordeaux Wine Course. Located in the middle of the French wine country. Also offers French courses. Contact B.L.S. 1 cours Georges-Clemenceau, 33000 Bordeaux; telephone: 05 56 51 00 76; fax: 05 56 51 76 15; e-mail: *bls@imaginet.fr;* website: *http://www.bls-bordeaux.com.*

Le Cordon Bleu. The most famous culinary institute in the world, Le Cordon Bleu began in Paris (though offshoots exist in other parts of the world). Master chefs train students from around the globe; diploma courses are available for professionals, though serious amateurs can take a ten-week course in the art of French cuisine with translations into English. Basic-, intermediate- and superior-level wine courses are also offered for serious amateurs and aspiring professionals. Contact U.S. Corporate Office: (800) 457-CHEF. Or in Paris: Le Cordon Bleu, 8, rue Léon Delhomme, 75015 Paris; *Métro:* Vaugirard; telephone: 01 53 68 22 50; fax: 01 48 56 03 77; website: *http://www.cordonbleu.net/textsite/school.htm.*

At Home with Patricia Wells: Cooking in Provence. An American in Paris and Provence, Patricia Wells is the International Herald Tribune's restaurant critic and author of several popular books on French cooking and bistros. She offers exclusive four- or five-day cooking programs at her eighteenth-century home in the south of France. Contact Judith Jones, 708 Sandown Place, Raleigh, North Carolina 27615; fax: (919) 846-2081; e-mail: *jj708@mindspring.com.*

Ritz Escoffier. This gourmet cooking school in Paris offers diploma and specialty courses and workshops. All courses are taught in French with English translation. Contact Ritz Paris, 15, Place Vendôme, 75041 Paris, Cedex 01; telephone 01 43 16 30 50; fax: 01 43 16 31 50; e-mail: *ecole@ ritzparis.com;* website: *http://www.ritz.com.*

Writing/Literature
WICE Paris Writer's Workshop. Held in the summer, this workshop brings together leading writers to discuss fiction, nonfiction, and poetry. Contact WICE, 20 boulevard du Montparnasse, 75015 Paris; *Métro*: Duroc or Falguière; telephone: 01 45 66 75 50; fax: 01 40 65 96 53; e-mail: *wice@club-internet.fr.*

International Inkwell. A retreat for writers that is located near the medieval city of Carcassonne, in the southwest of France. Five-day stays include sightseeing, candlelight dinners, and horseback riding. Contact Café du Livre, rue de la Mairie, 11170 Montolieu, Aude; telephone: 04 68 24 81 17; fax: 04 68 24 83 21; website: *http://www.pavilion.co.uk/valleverde.*

History
WICE. History comes alive on theme-oriented trips. Contact WICE, 20 boulevard du Montparnasse, 75015 Paris; *Métro*: Duroc or Falguière; telephone: 01 45 66 75 50; fax: 01 40 65 96 53; e-mail: *wice@club-internet.fr.*

Computers/Web Design
The American University of Paris (collaborating with Parsons Paris School of Design). Offers a six-week course. Contact The American University of Paris, Division of Continuing Education, 102, rue St. Dominique, 75007 Paris; telephone: 01 40 62 07 20; fax: 01 40 62 07 17; e-mail: *summer@aup.fr.*

ADVANCED DEGREES FOR ENGLISH SPEAKERS

Serious students can participate in numerous university degree programs in France that provide classes in English. International management is among the favorite topics, though many others are available. The following is a list of some universities with English-language studies:

General Studies
The American University of Paris. Offers an American-style university education with classes in English. Courses lead to a BA or BS degree. Located at 31, avenue Bosquet, 75007 Paris; telephone: 01 40 62 06 00; fax: 01 47 05 33 49.

European School of Management. A full-time International MBA course taught in English. Contact EAP-MBA office, 6, avenue de la Porte de Champerret, 75838 Paris, Cedex 17; telephone: 01 44 09 33 31; fax: 01 44 09 33 35; e-mail: *mba@eap.net*; website: *http://www.eap.net.*

Schiller International University. Offers an American-style university education including BBA, MBA, BA, and MA degrees. Specializes in international business and international relations and diplomacy. Full-time and part-time programs available. Contact Schiller International University, 32, boulevard de Vaugirard, 75015 Paris; telephone: 01 45 38 56 01; website: *http://www.schiller.edu.*

MBA Specialties

École des Hautes Études Internationales. Founded in 1899, this is the oldest French institute of international relations. Offers English-speaking programs that lead to an MA and PhD in international relations and diplomacy. Contact CEDS, 54, avenue Marceau 75008 Paris; telephone: 01 47 20 57 47; fax: 01 47 20 57 30; e-mail: *cepc@cepcnet.org.*

International Executive MBA/GA Institute of Technology. A course given at the Institute for American Universities in Aix-en-Provence. MBA accredited, offering a part-time eighteen-month program with a final three-week residency in Atlanta, Georgia. Contact IEMBA, IAU, 27, place de l'Université, 13625 Aix-en-Provence, Cedex 1; telephone: 04 42 23 39 35; e-mail: *iaumba@univ-aix.fr;* website: *http://www.iemba.iau.edu.*

ISG International School of Business. Offers an executive MBS with a part-time program or an intensive international MBA in three major economic zones: Paris, New York, and Tokyo. Contact ISG International School of Business, 45, rue Spontini, 75116 Paris; telephone: 01 56 26 11 07; fax: 01 56 26 11 06; e-mail: *isb@isg.fr;* website: *http://www.isg.fr.*

21
A Toast to Your Health

ASK WHO WANTS TO LIVE TO BE A HUNDRED, AND THE ANSWER IS
THE PERSON WHO IS NINETY-NINE.
—Betty Comden, *Break the Other Leg* (1994)

"*Santé*," says the Frenchman, gracefully lifting a glass of *vin rouge* high, just long enough to admire its luster before the contents float down his throat with a satisfying small slurp.

Wine is considered a health food in France—unless, that is, you're my husband's cardiologist, who limits his patients' wine intake to a half glass a day. It's quite an affront to the wine producers and anyone who values the pleasure of the proper Sancerre or Gigondas with a meal.

Most French ignore this advice and will remind you of the French paradox. That despite the flaky French croissants, the cheese trays filled with cholesterol, and the sauces that are ninety-nine percent butter, the French have a lower heart-attack rate than us so-called health nuts on the other side of the pond. Of course, there are those who also attribute the benefits to relaxed meals, fresh foods, and lots of walking.

France is also fortunate to have an excellent health-care system, which is based on a democratic system of socialized medicine that provides health-care access to all, with a personal attention that's extremely welcomed by anyone who's suffered through the HMO number-cruncher's system.

Various aspects of the system, however, operate differently, so we'll look at those aspects that tend to differ from what Americans are accustomed to.

Choosing Health-Care Providers

You can find a physician, dentist, or hospital in several ways. Ask at the local embassy or consulate, or ask an employer, neighbor, friends, or pharmacist. Finding a good French specialist can be as easy as asking your American physician to check his reference book, the *Directory of Medical Specialists*. This is how we got the name of that spoilsport cardiologist.

Physicians

French doctors are more approachable than their U.S. counterparts, quite literally since many of them, especially in small towns, act as their own receptionist and accounts-receivable departments. We still remember our confusion when our doctor handed us the bill after the visit, then collected the 100 francs on the spot. Why not? He was the only one in the office, and it was simpler that way. Since the bill was $17 for the forty-five minutes he'd spent with us, we complied happily.

Nonetheless, you will be expected to pay for extras and may even have to replace supplies, such as shots and sutures. When my husband cut his hand, he rushed to our doctor, who used his best embroidery technique to pull my husband back together with seven stitches. The doctor then handed him a prescription for the needle and sutures, which were packaged in a small kit at the pharmacy. We purchased it and returned it on the next visit, at which time the doctor stored our replacement kit among his supplies.

Doctors will make appointments with you, but many physicians also specify certain days and hours as general clinic times. You can simply show up without an appointment and wait your turn.

Home visits are not an anachronism in France. If you can't make it to the doctor's office, he can come to you, though he charges more for the service. The same is true for nurses, if you need regular shots or other treatments.

Doctors in France work in a rotating schedule whereby they cover for each other on their days off. If you call your doctor's office on his day off, the recording will provide the name of the doctor in charge that day. In many areas, the *medicin du garde* will be listed at the *mairie* or in the local paper.

Medical costs are extremely reasonable by American standards. A normal office visit with a general practitioner can cost just 100 FF to 130 FF (about $17 to $22). Specialist prices are higher, but not exorbitant.

Nurses and Midwives

Nurses, or *infirmieres*, work with doctors or on their own as special practitioners who visit the elderly or infirm at home. One American who broke his leg was treated every week by the nurse, who arrived punctually enough to spoil his afternoon happy hour.

Maternity care is often provided by *sages-femmes*, or midwives, who act as mother hens. Children are born for the most part in the hospitals or clinics.

Dental Care
One thing we have noticed about Europe, and France in particular, is the sad state of teeth. We don't know why this is the case, since the dental care we've received has been fine. However, you'll want to take charge of care by insisting on your regular cleaning. Having tartar removed is called *détartrage* and the method used is ultrasound, a highly popular and quick way of removing tartar. Five minutes and you're done.

The bill is equally enjoyable. Our last dental visit included two cleanings for my husband and me, and filling a small cavity. The total came to 222 FF ($37).

Don't expect the dentist to send handy reminders for cleanings. Marketing is still frowned upon in French medical and dental circles. My dentist was shocked when I suggested it. Reminding people to come back was too much like pressuring them to spend money on dentistry. "When they need it," he said, "they'll call me."

Eyeglasses/Contact Lenses
An optometrist is an *opticien* in France. In the major Paris stores, you can get your glasses in an hour, but expect a longer wait in the countryside. If you are in serious need of vision correction, bring an extra pair of glasses and/or contact lenses with you. Also bring a copy of your eye prescription, so you can purchase replacements.

Pharmacies and Prescriptions
The pharmacist plays a vital role in France, much more so than in the United States. Not only can the pharmacy fill a doctor's prescriptions, but the pharmacist can also diagnose simple problems and supply the necessary drugs. When the flu hits in France, it's the pharmacist who's on the frontline of the fight. French pharmacies also provide homeopathic, natural solutions, such as special teas under the name of *homeopathie*. During the fall, the pharmacist will even tell mushroom hunters if their harvest is safe to eat.

Prescriptions from the United States won't be honored in France. However, bring your pills in the original containers or a prescription using the drug's generic name, as well as the trade name and the dosage. The doctor will know what you're taking and be able to supply the same or an equivalent medication. Our only problem in this regard was the reverse case. When we returned for a lengthy visit to the States, a medication prescribed by my husband's French cardiologist was not available in the States.

We were obliged to have a friend in France visit the pharmacist and mail the medicine to us.

Your French doctor or dentist will provide prescriptions for medicine and for tests at the laboratories (*laboratoires*). In the latter case, you have the test done, then return to pick up the results yourself. The results show the norms for the test, the actual results, and where the results stand in relation to the norm. The doctor usually receives a faxed copy, and sometimes you'll be requested to call the doctor to discuss the results.

The pharmacy is indicated by a large green cross. If it's lit, the pharmacy is open. Normal hours are Monday through Saturday, though in small towns individual pharmacies may be closed Monday or Tuesday. As with small shops, pharmacies are run by individuals and often close during the lunch "hour," which is usually from noon to two. Pharmacies post the address of the nearest pharmacy in charge (*pharmacie de garde*) when they are closed. The list is also published in the local newspaper and listed in the information guides for residents. The guides are supplied by the town hall.

Hospitals and Clinics

The biggest difference between French hospitals and their U.S. counterparts is that the French don't rush patients in and out like a revolving door. When someone's ill enough to need hospitalization or surgery, the doctors feel an obligation to keep them until they're perfectly capable of being at home alone. My husband's cardiologist's eyebrows reached Eiffel Tower height when we commented that the procedure John was about to undergo was performed on an outpatient basis in the States. "But how can they prepare and monitor?" he asked, shaking his head at the folly of *les Americains*. My husband stayed the requisite three days. Incidentally, the cost was a third of what the outpatient procedure would have been in the States.

The French hospital system includes both public and private hospitals. The hospital system is divided according to intensity of care needed: short-, medium-, or long-term stays. The short-stay hospitals are for people undergoing surgery. Those convalescing from surgery, who require further rest—for example, after hip replacement or open-heart surgery—are transferred to a medium-stay hospital for recuperation, physical therapy, or as was the case with a woman friend who lived alone, simply for the chance to heal her hip sufficiently to maneuver alone in her home.

Long-term centers are for those who cannot care for themselves without aid and although not solely for elderly, are much like nursing homes.

A public regional hospital is a *Centre Hospitalier Régional*, or CHR for short. If a hospital is related to a university as a teaching hospital, it's indicated by the name *Centre Hospitalier Universitaire*, or CHU for short. A private hospital (*hôpital*) or clinic (*clinique*) provides specialized care, such as maternity or orthopedics. The cost is higher in private settings.

The American Hospital of Paris permits Americans to pay with dollars, and they accept Blue Cross-Blue Shield. The address is 63, boulevard Victor Hugo, 92202 Neuilly-sur-Seine Cedex; telephone: 01 46 41 25 25. Another English-speaking hospital is the Hertford British Hospital, 3, rue Barbès, 82300 Lavallois-Perret; telephone: 01 47 58 133 12.

LE BON MOT: HEALTH CARE

Common complaints

Grippe..................	Flu
Mal de tête	Headache
Rhume	Cold
Toux	Cough

Prescriptions

Comprimé..............	Tablet
Contre-indication	Warning
Effets secondaire	Side effect
Pilule.................	Pill

Doctor Visits

Examen................	Physical exam
Feuille de soins	Receipt (for health care)
Ordonnance	Prescription
Rendez-vous	Appointment

Emergency Services

The first few pages of French phone directories list numbers to call in emergencies, *Services d'Urgence et d'Assistance* (see chapter 15). When you arrive in France, put the local ambulance, police, and fire numbers near your phone. Numbers are also provided for poison control and special help organizations. Paris has various other numbers such as *SOS Médicins,* 01 47 07 77 77, and *SOS Dentistes,* 01 43 37 51 00, for twenty-four-hour medical or dental care.

A big difference in emergency services in France involves the fire fighters (*pompiers*). They are also highly trained first-aid workers (*sapeurs*), who are proud of their abilities and are usually listed under the combined term, *pompier/sapeurs.* They provide emergency first aid. They are usually the ones to be called for medical emergencies as well as fires. Among other things, they have cardiac and resuscitation equipment and the training to stabilize heart-attack victims.

Ambulance services are for nonemergencies and used mainly for transporting an ill person from home to hospital and back or from a surgery hospital to a long-term stay clinic. They will also have first aid and oxygen. For this service, call the municipal ambulance service (*ambulances municipals*) or a private company, which often does double duty as a taxi service. They're listed in the yellow pages.

Don't call a municipal ambulance for a heart attack. Call the emergency numbers.

MEDICAL INSURANCE

To live in France, you must prove that you have health-care coverage. Check your current health insurer to see if the company will provide this coverage. If you will be overseas for a short time, they may cover you. However, you'll be required to pay the bills (unless it's from the American Hospital in Paris, which treats U.S. patients as if they are within its borders), then apply for reimbursement. This takes forever. Despite pre-approvals and such, we never got reimbursed without twelve phone calls and a final desperate attempt of a letter to the U.S. state's insurance commissioner.

If your U.S. insurance won't provide health coverage overseas, you can buy an expatriate health-care policy or use French insurance, if you are a resident. The latter requires proof of residence, such as your *visa de long séjour*.

Several insurance companies in Europe provide coverage for people outside their native country—the country for which they hold a passport. These expatriate policies usually provide a tier of prices, ranging from the cheapest European coverage only, to worldwide coverage (excepting the United States), to the most expensive policy that includes the United States.

Note that Medicare does not cover health care overseas. You'll need other coverage in France. If you're over sixty-five, contact the American Association of Retired Persons for information about foreign medical coverage that offers Medicare supplement plans.

If you reside legally in France and are working, you can be part of the French *Sécurité Sociale (Sécu)*. You will pay into the system and be covered by their policy, which covers a percentage of health care and prescriptions. You can buy supplement policies to this, as well, since *Sécurité Sociale* does not cover the full bill. (EU citizens with national health plans can cover their health needs via the reciprocal agreement between EU countries.)

Even if you're not working in France, if you reside in the country and have a *carte de séjour*, you can apply for a medical insurance policy under *Sécurité Sociale*. Contact one of the offices for information.

Expatriate Insurance Plans

Companies (and one broker) that provide health insurance coverage to American expatriates include the following.

Advantage Insurance Associates brokers health, motor, home, disability, and business risk insurance. Although the company is a subentity of a French insurance consulting firm, it was set up by an American specifically to work with the large American expatriate community in Paris and other parts France. All correspondence is in English. The company insures a number of personnel from the American embassy in Paris. Contact AIA at 57, rue du Faubourg de Montmartre, 75009 Paris; telephone: 01 53.20.03.33.

Blue Cross and Blue Shield of Western Europe. Offers American-style health insurance plans, which may be costlier than some European plans; but if you already have a current Blue Cross insurance plan in the States, you can transfer into the Western Europe plan without a physical exam and transfer back to the U.S. plan on your return—with no preexisting condition exclusion period. This plan provides direct billing and advice in English. Contact BCBS of Western Europe at 59, rue de Châteaudun, 75009 Paris; telephone: 33 1 42 81 98 76; fax 33 1 42 81 99 03.

BUPA International. BUPA is one of the largest overseas health-care insurers specializing in health insurance for individuals and their families who live and work outside their home country. Contact BUPA at Russell Mews, Brighton, Great Britain BN7 2NR, United Kingdom; UK telephone: 44 1273 208 181; UK fax: 44 1273 866 583.

ExpaCare Insurance Services. Offers a StandardCare Plan for hospitalization and emergency transport and a more comprehensive SpecialCare Plan for outpatient and other costs. Works with International SOS to provide twenty-four-hours-a-day multilingual assistance. Contact ExpaCare at Dukes Court, Duke Street, Woking, Surrey GU21 5XB, England; UK telephone: 44 1483 717 800; UK fax: 44 1483 776 620.

International Health Insurance Danmark a/s. Owned by Denmark's largest national health-insurance company and insures expats of all nationalities in more than 140 countries. They offer several choices of health plans to cover hospitals, doctors, medicine, and ambulance transport. Dental, spectacles/contact lens coverage, and medical evacuation insurance are also available. Contact at 64a Athol Street, Douglas, Isle of Man, United Kingdom, IM1 1JE; UK telephone: 44 1624 677 412.

Lloyds Expatriate Protection Plan. England's oldest insurance syndicate offers health insurance specifically designed for people living outside the country for which they hold a passport. Coverage for medical expenses is based on the area of the world where you intend to use it. People up to age seventy-five are eligible. Call their U.S. toll-free number (800) 399-3904; website: *www.artitude.com/costa*.

PPP International Health Plan. One of the United Kingdom's leading medical-insurance companies, with over two million members. The International Division specializes in insurance for people working or living overseas and includes full-refund emergency evacuation service. Contact them at Phillips House, Crescent Road, Tunbridge Wells, Kent, TN1 2PL; UK telephone: 44 1892 512 345; UK fax: 44 1892 515 143.

The above list is by no means all-inclusive. Several other insurance companies in Paris specialize in serving English speakers in France. For additional names, check a current issue of *FUSAC* or the *Paris Voice*.

In addition, several expatriate groups offer policies to their members. Among them are American Citizens Abroad (ACA) and the Association of Americans Resident Overseas (AARO).

Contact ACA at 5 bis rue Liotard, CH-1202 Geneva, Switzerland; telephone: (41-22) 340 0233; e-mail: *acage@aca.ch*; website: *http://www.aca.ch*.

Contact AARO at B.P. 127, 92154 Suresnes Cedex; telephone: 01 42 04 09 38; fax 01 42 04 09 12; e-mail: *aaroparis@aol.com*; website: *http://members.aol.com/aaroparis/aarohome.htm*.

> *Like many, many Americans living abroad, I may come limping back home*
> *by the time I am a geriatric case, since we are not covered by Medicare abroad.*
>
> —Dorothy, Haute-Savoie

SECURITY

While there are certainly cases of murder and mayhem suitable for Hercule Poirot, France is a civilized country and not particularly dangerous. In fact, gun-related deaths are vastly fewer in France than in the United States, not counting of course, deer and rabbit and an occasional wine-loaded hunter during hunting season.

Your car and wallet are the main targets. Be particularly wary at tourist sites and anywhere in Paris, especially *le Métro*. My husband came home beaming one day because he'd foiled a pair of pickpockets. One had "accidentally" dropped his ticket in front of my husband when getting on the *Métro*, while the other pushed against my husband's hip pocket. John's wallet was safely stowed in another pocket, which was buttoned and underneath a pack he was carrying. Often, in high-theft areas, John carries his passport in a security pouch under his shirt.

My own special trick is to carry real valuables, such as passport, credit cards, and large sums of money, in the hidden compartment of my shoulder purse with the strap worn crosswise. I tuck small change and a bill or two in a pocket so that it's handy for minor purchases on the street such as water or postcards. This avoids having to advertise the presence and location of the real stash.

Lock your vehicle and never leave your belongings visible. If you must leave luggage or valuables in the car, put them in the trunk and lock it before you arrive at the destination. When you arrive at the destination, lock the car normally and walk away as though nothing's in the car.

Most streets in Paris and other large cities are populated at night and, if you stick to these areas, you'll feel more comfortable. But be aware where you're walking and don't wander down dark, empty areas.

For the most part, just relax and enjoy being in France.

22
Of Bloodlines and Loopholes

Sad to say, wine and roses occasionally defer to death and taxes. In previous chapters, we talked about taxes on your TV and taxes on your car and taxes on your house and taxes on earnings.

Now it's time to discuss inheritance taxes and other details related to that dreaded final voyage. I'm not trying to spoil your good time, but it's better for your finances and heirs if you're aware of certain strange situations, including a dastardly little detail regarding French inheritance regulations and the rights of survivors.

FRENCH INHERITANCE LAWS

Hold onto your berets, because most Americans don't believe this, but French law stipulates that blood relatives must inherit specific portions of your estate, whether house, stocks, cash, or other valuables.

A spouse is not a blood relative—or at least not unless you have a very strange family. Translated, this means that, even if the husband or wife has worked all his or her life to help accumulate that tidy estate, the surviving spouse often does not have a right to inherit it. French regulations state that specific portions (*réserve legale*) of an estate must first go to children, then to the parents, grandparents, siblings, cousins, and their children. The remainder (*quotité disponible*), which depends on the number of blood relatives, can be left to the spouse or whomever the deceased wishes to name.

For example, if the deceased has one child, French law currently states that the child must inherit at least half of the estate. Two children must inherit at least two-thirds. If the children number three or more, they must share a minimum of three-fourths of the estate.

If the deceased had no children, then the estate goes to parents at a rate of twenty-five percent per parent. Brothers and sisters also receive a portion, but can be disinherited, if the will so specifies it.

The remainder of the estate, once this reserved portion has been accounted for, is free or disposable (*disponible*) and can be willed as the deceased wishes. Thus, if a couple has three children and those children inherit the required seventy-five percent, the spouse can inherit the remaining twenty-five percent.

The French themselves don't like this regulation, most particularly the increasing population of working women who watch their kids take off to Club Med with the money. The *code civil* is currently being studied for possible reform—but it has been studied for years, so no promises are being made. While waiting for more sane inheritance regulations, pay particular attention to protecting your estate and your spouse.

One solution used by French couples is to protect their spouses with insurance, so they have the means to live after the kids inherit the estate. Others insert a special clause in their house contract (*clause tontine*), which allows the property to be left to the survivor. This must be done when you purchase the property. Still others make a gift between spouses (*donation entre époux*), which gives the survivor the use of the home as long as they live.

> Some couples only have one set of kids, their own,
> so maybe they don't care so much. But in second marriages like ours,
> with his and her kids, it [French inheritance law] makes you worry
> that you'll be left out in the cold.
> —Diana, Loire Valley

Marital Regime and Property

A clause in a property purchase contract enables a couple to change what the French call the *régime matrimonial*. The *régime* defines whether a couple's property is held jointly (*communauté universelle*) or separately (*séparation des biens*). In the latter case, each keeps property that is inherited or owned before marriage, but jointly own assets, such as a house, acquired after marriage.

You can legally change your *régime*, and may want to do so if you buy property in France as a couple. At that time, the *notaire* will ask you which *régime* you were married under and if you had a marriage contract. Hmmm...for Americans this is a puzzlement, since most of us weren't married in France. To find the answer, check the regulations of the state where you were married. Usually, without a marriage contract, you're assumed to be married based on the joint ownership of assets. If you want to change this, tell the *notaire*.

The *notaire* or lawyer (*avocat*) will help you set up and sign the legal forms required. Again, make sure these arrangements are made prior to signing a purchase contract for property, because the house ownership and purchase contract should reflect your wishes.

Whatever you do, consult a *notaire* or lawyer who is familiar with the various inheritance and tax laws. These are extremely complicated in France and should not be left to chance. Lawyers familiar with both American and French law tend to be located in Paris, though you may be able to find someone in other areas who can answer your questions and handle the situation. Talk to several *notaires* and ask about their experience in dealing with contracts and wills for Americans.

WILLS

A French will is called a *testament*. France recognizes two main types of wills: a simple handwritten will (*testament olographe*), and an official will (*testament authentique*) as written by a *notaire* or lawyer.

The handwritten will must literally be in your handwriting (not typed or written on a computer), dated, and signed. You can create this type of will, as long as your will is simple and meets French regulations for specific portions of the estate to be left to relatives based on the legal ranking (*réserve legale*). Even if you do the handwritten will yourself, leave a copy of it with a *notaire* or lawyer.

If your situation is at all complicated or you need to change your marital *régime*, you'll need the help of a *notaire* or lawyer in putting together a will. They will help you draft an official will, or a *testament authentique*. A copy of this will stay in the professional's office.

You can have an American will and a French will. Just be sure that the French will mentions the American one and vice versa, making it clear that your estate will be handled separately in the two countries.

Whether you choose to make France or the United States your fiscal residence has serious tax and inheritance ramifications. Get professional advice and, if you don't understand something, keep asking questions until you do.

Reporting a Death

Deaths involving expatriates in France must be reported to the appropriate consulate or embassy. Burial can take place in either country, though the expense of shipping the remains, of course, increases the cost, leaving all the less for portioning among the ranks of blood relatives.

INHERITANCE TAXES

As in the United States, taxes are paid on inheritance in France. These taxes apply whether the deceased is a resident or nonresident, however; the country to which you pay these taxes will depend on your legal residence at the time of death.

Your legal domicile (*domicile fiscile*) will become France if you meet any of the following qualifications: You live in France for more than half the year (183 days); your family and principal home are in France; you work or have vital investments or a business in France.

If you're not considered a resident of France, then your inheritance taxes would be paid in the United States (unless you've chosen another country), except for taxes on property that's physically located in France.

If you're judged to be domiciled in France, each person who inherits from your estate, no matter where they live, pays French inheritance tax. The rate depends on the relationship between the deceased and beneficiary, all of which is strictly regulated by French law.

The surviving spouse is allowed 330,000 FF (about $55,000) as an allowance prior to taxes being assessed. Children and parents have an allowance of 300,000 FF (about $50,000). Beyond this amount, taxes are based on a sliding scale ranging from five percent for amounts up to 50,000 FF to forty percent on assets more than 11.2 million FF. The same situation is applicable for other relatives, with various levels of allowances and tax rates.

The necessary paperwork is usually prepared by a *notaire*, who files a tax return on the estate within six months of the death or within twelve months, if the death occurred outside France. You do not need to file a tax return if the estate is valued at less than 10,000 FF and the sole beneficiary is a spouse.

In France, even more so than in the United States, it's essential to plan in advance for the inevitable—especially prior to buying property or making serious investments.

To Be or Not to Be a Resident

Many Americans who move to France as adults keep their money in the United States and maintain ties there, including an address, a business, and a family. You can sometimes use these ties to build the case that you are in

France temporarily, rather than as a permanent resident, thus maintaining your domicile in the United States, should you care to do so.

If you do not officially live full-time in France, then French estate taxes and inheritance laws can be avoided, except for taxes on property, such as a house and checking account, within France. Usually, if you live in France for the full 183 days a year, you will be considered domiciled there unless you meet other tests; for example, employees on specific work assignments, who maintain obvious ties to the United States may be exempt.

The regulations are complex. Talk to a lawyer to determine how to best proceed and whether to establish domicile in France.

Your Best Defense
Every situation is different, and French laws are so extensive and complicated that while setting up our purchase contract and marital *régime*, I got the impression that even our *notaire* wasn't sure what the ruling was. (In fact, he didn't know and had to consult higher state authorities in the outer reaches of Paris.) I urge you to get the best advice you can when it comes to your tax and inheritance situation.

Due to the strange French inheritance and tax laws, I intend to simply run
for the plane heading to the States as soon as I feel the heart attack coming on.
—Bill, Loire Valley

23
Retracing Your Steps

BREATHES THERE THE MAN, WITH SOUL SO DEAD...
WHOSE HEART HATH NE'ER WITHIN HIM BURN'D
AS HOME HIS FOOTSTEPS HE HATH TURN'D
FROM WANDERING ON A FOREIGN STRAND!
—Sir Walter Scott (1771–1832)

Returning to the United States after your adventure in France is mainly a reverse of the procedures you followed to get here. That is not the main problem. Most people who've returned to the States from a stay overseas, whether in France or elsewhere, cite the transition back to the United States as being as difficult—or worse—than the move to France.

In any case, you will return to a different place, both physically and mentally. Even if you return to the same city or suburb you left, daily life there will have gone on without you. Your family, friends, and neighbors have moved on while you were gone, and you can't just plop yourself back in the same hole you left. They will know the current movies, books, and popular culture. When they refer to them in conversation, you'll feel lost in a time warp.

You also may compare the two cultures and find that there were things you now appreciate about France that you didn't previously realize was a problem in the States. Traffic, violence, and fast foods may suddenly compare unfavorably to your French lifestyle. And if you voice any of these distinctions, your friends may respond in confusion or anger.

On the positive side, you may thoroughly enjoy being back where you can speak easily without worrying about all those verb tenses and nouns.

Give yourself time to adjust. Don't assume that because this is your home country, you won't have a problem.

I'll be happy going back, falling back into my same job.
My father's ill, so I'll be excited to be back for my family. [But] I wouldn't
trade this [a year living in Paris] for anything....It's been a good experience for us.
—Amanda, Paris

MOVING IN REVERSE

Hopefully you were pleased with the movers who originally handled your move. If so, contact their representative in France to arrange your belongings' return journey.

If this is not an option, you can find the names of international movers through friends, classified ads in *FUSAC*, or listings in the yellow pages. Paris is packed with moving companies that are familiar with the requirements for moving abroad. Just be sure you interview several companies and get estimates for the cost and volume of container they expect you will need.

A few of the movers that are associated with American companies are listed here.

Desbordes International is one of the largest companies; their vans and cargo trucks are seen on roads throughout France. The company has English-speaking staff, provides storage, customs clearance, and pet and car shipping. They're associated with Mayflower, United Van Lines, Atlas Van Lines, and other American companies. Contact: Desbordes International, 12-14, rue de la Véga 75012 Paris; telephone: 01 44 73 84 84; fax: 01 43 42 51 48; e-mail: *info@desbordesinternational.com*; website: *http://www.desbordesinternational.com.*

Grospiron International is associated with United Van Lines, Mayflower, and Atlas Van Lines among others. Telephone in Paris: 01 48 11 71 71 or Lyon: 04 72 47 38 90; e-mail: *info@grospiron.com*; website: *http://www. grospiron.com.*

Biard International, 72 rue Maurice Ripoche, 75014 Paris; telephone: 01 49 61 90 30; fax: 01 49 61 14 39.

Two of our [American] friends moved back to the States, because they didn't like
France; but I do like it...the lifestyle, history, difference. So it'll be strange to go back.
—Pam, Le Mans

Stateside Customs

The United States Customs Service has regulations regarding what you can import back to the States. There is no limit on the total amount of money you can bring into France or take back to the States with you. But if you take out or bring in more than $10,000, you must file a report, Customs Form 4790, with U.S. Customs. The money can be in U.S. or foreign currency, traveler's checks, money orders, or investment securities. Of course, you can have large amounts of money, such as that received from selling a house in France, wired from your French bank to a bank account in the States. In this case, the financial institution handles the paperwork.

For full information on the customs regulations, request the booklet *Know Before You Go: Customs Regulations for U.S. Residents* from the U.S. Customs Service. The American embassy has copies of this overseas. You can also visit the U.S. Customs website at *http://www.customs.ustreas.gov.*

Remember Pets

You may assume that your pets came originally from the States so they can return easily. But once they moved overseas, they have to meet the same regulations as any pets you may acquire in France. These are basically the same regulations as those required on entering France, meaning that cats and dogs must be free of any diseases that can be communicated to man.

Dogs older than three months must be vaccinated for rabies at least thirty days prior to entry into the United States, but no more than twelve months prior. Proof of vaccination must be shown with the veterinarian's signature. You may also need a certificate of good health from the veterinarian signed within three days of your entry.

Pet birds are subject to quarantine, which requires advance reservations. Request current regulations when you are ready to return. These are listed in the leaflet, *Pets, Wildlife, U.S. Customs*, which is available from the U.S. Customs Service or from embassies overseas.

> *It was strange to go back [to the States]...easy to go back in business,*
> *but psychologically a tremendous change. We never forgot France and*
> *finally decided to pick up and return here.*
> —Sara, Vernoux

Treasure the Memories

Once you've tasted the life in France, it may agree with you. Some people never return, though most do eventually. Either way, I hope that you've reaped enjoyment from your sojourn here.

The advantages of having lived in France endure longer than your stay. Living in France will be a cherished memory, and I hope it's one that has left you with a wonderful *joie de vivre.*

Resources

MIGHTY RIVERS CAN EASILY BE LEAPED AT THEIR SOURCE.
—Publilius Syrus, *Moral Saying*

The following sources can help you gather specific information and answer questions related to your interests and situation in moving to France. For a list of social groups that can help you begin adapting to the new life and make new friends, refer to chapter 6 (see page 47).

FRENCH GOVERNMENT AND TOURISM

French Embassy, 4101 Reservoir Road NW, Washington, D.C. 20007-2185; telephone: (202) 944-6 ; fax: (202) 944-6212 (visa section).

Paris Tourism Office, 127, avenue des Champs-Elysées, 75008 Paris. *Métro:* Charles-de-Gaulle Etoile, George V. (Additional branches at Louvre, Gare du Nord, Gare de Lyon, and the Eiffel Tower); telephone: 01 49 52 53 54; fax: 01 49 52 53 00. Website: *http://www.paris-promotion.fr/.*

French Government Tourist Office/U.S. Information requests: (202) 659-7779. New York Office: 444 Madison Avenue, 16th Floor, New York, NY 10022-6903; fax: (212) 838-7855. Chicago Office: 676 N. Michigan Avenue, Chicago, IL 60611-2819; fax: (312) 337-6339. Los Angeles Office: 9454 Wilshire Blvd., Suite 715, Beverly Hills, CA 90212-2967; fax: (310) 276-2835.

AMERICAN AND BRITISH GOVERNMENT

United Kingdom, 35, rue Faubourg St. Honoré, Paris; telephone: 01 42 66 91 42.

United States Embassy, 2, avenue Gabriel, Paris; telephone: 01 43 12 22 22.

On-Line Connections

The following websites are just the start of possibilities for gathering information on any topic you may be interested in regarding France. They're divided into their main category of interest and information, though many of these sites include extensive links to other sites. Once you start researching, the web extends to the farthest reaches of French culture, language, practical details, and personal contacts.

Tourist/Travel Information

U.S. State Department/Consular Affairs. Provides access to passport and visa information and travel warnings. Website: *http://travel.state.gov.*

Language, Culture, and Travel

Bonjour Paris. A loose assortment of articles on various Paris activities and culture, basically whatever their authors wanted to discuss, plus some simple French lessons. Website: *http://www.bparis.com.*

Country Net. Practical information on taxes, real estate agents, and much more, all specifically designed for people relocating to countries around the world. The service charges a fee, but permits a free trial period of two weeks, which may be all you'll need. Website: *http://www.countrynet.com.*

National Federation of Tourist Offices provides information on traveling in France. Website: *http://www.tourisme.fr.*

French Regions. provides a range of interesting information on history, culture, and activities in various areas of France. Website: *http://www. france.com.*

French Links. A "cultural connection," by Rachel Kaplan, who is self-promoting her books and tours; some of the web links come in handy. Website: *http://www.frenchlinks.com.*

Travlang's Foreign Language for Travelers. Tips and translations for various languages around the world. Website: *http://www.travlang.com/languages/.*

Expatriate Groups

American Citizens Abroad (ACA). Provides news, information, and tips relevant to Americans living abroad. Website: *http://www.aca.ch.*

Association of Americans Resident Overseas (AARO). Information and relevant legislation pertaining to Americans overseas. Website: *http://www. members.aol.com/aaroparis/aarohome.htm.*

Index